Linda McCullough Thew left school at 14 to work in the village store described in this book. In 1942 she joined the ATS in which she worked on anti-aircraft radar. She transferred to the Army Education Corps and subsequently took a teachers' training course in Newcastle. After a career teaching in a number of schools and counselling, Linda McCullough Thew turned to full-time writing. Her work has been broadcast, she has written short stories and is at present engaged on a novel. This is her first full-length book.

Ashington Industrial Co-operative Society was first registered in 1893 by a group of working people anxious to emulate the success of the Rochdale Pioneers and many other co-operatives which by that time had become firmly established in most industrial towns and cities. By the 1920s the Society was soundly based with a membership of around 10,000 people all owing a stake in the business and sharing its profits when a 'divi' was distributed. From premises in the centre of Ashington the Co-op prospered and extended into the surrounding area, opening a dozen branches.

The Society maintained its independence until 1970 when it was one of a number of small co-ops which banded together to form the North Eastern Co-operative Society, which has subsquently developed into one of the strongest and most successful regional co-operatives.

Linda McCullough Thew

The Pit Village and the Store

Pluto  Press

London and Sydney

in association with the Co-operative Union

First published in 1985 by Pluto Press Limited,
The Works, 105a Torriano Avenue, London NW5 2RX
and Pluto Press Australia Limited, PO Box 199, Leichhardt,
New South Wales 2040, Australia

7 6 5 4 3 2 1

89 88 87 86 85

Phototypeset by AKM Associates (UK) Ltd
Ajmal House, Hayes Road, Southall, Greater London
Printed in Great Britain by Guernsey Press Co. Limited
Guernsey, C.I.

British Library Cataloguing in Publication Data
Thew, Linda McCullough
The pit village and the store.
1. Coal miners——England——Northumberland
2. Northumberland——Social life and customs
I. Title
942.8'8082   DA670.N8

ISBN 0 7453 0069 3

Contents

Acknowledgements

I should like to thank my husband, Bill, and my son, Malcolm, for their work and co-operation in helping me illustrate this book.

I should also like to thank Launcelot Barnfather Summers for his help regarding information about the early days of Ashington Store together with Arthur Summers and Ross Miles for their help regarding work at the pit.

Dedication

To my father, Archie Summers, my mother, Margaret Summers, my brother, Bill Summers and the two of the younger generation who, with a wide field of choice before them, decided to follow the family tradition and work in the mines; my nephew, David Summers and my son, Malcolm McCullough

1. Ashington

'Hinny, ye shud nivvor gan past the store.'

And we almost never did.

The store in question was the Ashington Industrial Co-operative Society Limited, whose main premises were in the mining village of Ashington, Northumberland. Here I was to have my first job; in Ashington I was to pass my childhood.

In 1844, when the first store was opened in Rochdale, Ashington was a farm set in the Northumbrian countryside of whin, heather, trees and farmland. In 1846 the first lease to mine coal was given and three years later a shaft was sunk at Felham Down. For a quarter of a century this area was known as Fell-em Doon and it was here that the first miners' houses were erected.

Sinking a shaft

First store in Rochdale

By 1861, the population of Ashington and Sheepwash had reached 76. At that time, miners were skilled men who moved to new areas as each pit was worked out. Because of their semi-itinerant ways, they quickly settled down in any new environment. One such was my great-grandfather who, together with his wife and child and a bundle, left Tarry, a small pit near Eglingham, in the late 1860s. (Tarry was so named because they boiled their own barrels of tar, that is, they had their own methods of taking oil from their coal and boiling it to produce pitch or tar.) This working-man Dick Whittington walked to the mainline railway where he took the train from Alnwick to Morpeth. From Morpeth station, they walked to Fell-em-Doon. Whether their bundle represented their worldly possessions or whether these were to follow, or whether they came prepared to buy furniture for their new house, I cannot say. The child did not survive long. My grandfather, the younger brother, was born in Ashington in 1870, and so became the eldest son.

The earliest settlers in this district, those who came in the mid-1850s, were allocated one of the seven houses already built in Cross Row or one of the few completed in Long Row. If, for some reason, they could not get into a house immediately on their arrival, they spent a night or two in the 'Swankey Shop'. This was either temporary accommodation, or, more likely, a house with no furniture or bedding.

The first houses were simple back-to-back affairs. They were very poorly ventilated and this made them stiflingly hot in summer. In these hot summer evenings the small community took to the shade of a nearby wood or congregated on the grass, the children to play, the adults to chat. The women brought their knitting with them. Later, the coal owners were prevailed upon to do away with the back-to-back dwellings and Cross Row was gradually emptied and restructured for other tenants.

The Duke of Portland, who owned the land, attempted to restrict the number of roads, paths and fields which could be used by this growing community; to this end he put up signs saying 'No Road This Way'. It does not seem that they were very effective.

From the beginnings, more and more houses were built as near to the pit yard as possible. These were called 'Rows'. They were uniformly constructed in long straight lines, the longest having four blocks (sections), the shortest two. The first shops were opened in the houses of people living in these Rows. Further shops were built in Ashington Market Place, then the hub of the community and later to be called 'The High Market'.

Private houses and working-men's clubs were also built in fairly large numbers. The working-men's clubs were, of course, for men only. They provided places for men to go, not only to drink, but to chat and follow a particular hobby such as leek growing. Those in charge of the clubs said they helped control unruly behaviour caused by drink because members were ejected from the club and their membership terminated if they were guilty of indecorum.

Some very attractive cottages were built to house retired miners and their wives. One old lady, a Mrs Dunn who was born at Coneygarth, wrote:

I thank God for my cottage home
So kindly lent to me
By the miners of Northumberland
On whom God's blessing be.

In the early days the roads were water-logged and 'clarty' except when they were in the iron grip of winter. There were no street lights and people walking abroad in the dark hours carried lanterns. Houses were lit by oil-lamps suspended from the ceiling and by candles.

The water used by the inhabitants was provided at first by the pit and had to be chlorinated to be rendered fit for drinking. This gave it an unpleasant taste so the people bought water that had come a distance, for which they paid a halfpenny or a penny per pail. An ale house in the district charged a penny for a pail a beer. This beer wasn't strong enough for some drinkers, so they added more yeast and allowed it to ferment to give it more body.

In 1867 another shaft, Bothal Down Cast, was sunk. Tiny flickering spots of light could be seen by those curious enough to look down the shaft. These spots of light were the candles used by the bricklayers as they worked sitting on 'rope' seats suspended from the top of the shaft. When the coal was finally reached there was a grand celebration, a barrel of beer and a quantity of beef being provided (presumably by the mine owners) for the occasion.

Two fatal accidents marred the early history of Fell-em-Doon. Robert Brown lost his life falling from the pit heap and a young driver, William Temple, was killed while working down the pit. He left a widow and two children. There was no compensation as such in those days, but the mine owners were not unaware of the plight of the young woman now responsible for the upbringing of a young family. They bought her a mangle that she might take in washing and allowed her to sell gunpowder to the miners from the magazine that stood near the railway.

In those days, when there was an accident at the pit, the injured man was brought up and laid on a flat cart when he was jolted over the cobbled roads to his home. Usually, his wife would have been informed of the accident before he arrived there. 'Missus. There's been a fall of stone and your man's gettin' hissel hurt,' the harbinger of news would probably say.

When there was a fatal accident, the buzzer blew and all work in that particular area stopped. The men, solemn and begrimed, came silently up off the coal face. The sound of the buzzer blowing at a time other than that officially recognized, struck foreboding in the hearts of all who heard it. Work would stop as, one by one, housewives and those at home silently came to the door and waited for the approach of the flat cart.

In front of the cart walked the deputy. Behind it, in sombre procession, all the men who had been working with the dead man. When they arrived at the house of the bereaved the cortège would stop. All the men would remove their pit hats and the deputy would go forward to the wife and say, 'Missus. I'm awful sorry to have to tell you your man's been killed. Fall of stone. There was nowt we could do.'

She would not cry but her words would say it all. 'Eh. Me canny, canny man.' Then, 'Fetch him in, hinny.'

Automatically, her neighbours would rally round her. Some

would take her children and look after them for the time being, others would wash and prepare the dead man for his last resting place.

At this time, of course, there was little provision for people who were ill or men hurt at the pit. Nursing was done at home by the women of the family or, later, by trained nurses paid for by regular contributions from the miners. This state of affairs continued until 1915, when Ashington Hospital was built and subsequently maintained by donations from the people of Ashington and a levy from the miners. Mr Jonathan Priestman had become chairman and managing owner of the pits in the area, and it was his ideals that shaped the lifestyle of early Ashington. He believed strongly in the Quaker principles of looking after and caring for the workforce both in and out of working hours. No intoxicating liquors were sold. The first two hotels to be built were both temperance hotels. By the time the population reached 4,000 there was still only one policeman in Ashington. His was not an arduous job, for there was little drunkenness and even less crime. And with the growing prosperity of Ashington came all the developments to sustain its community – schools, churches and pastimes to fill the inhabitants' few leisure hours.

The first school was situated in the last house on Cross Row and doubled as a Methodist meeting-place, for links between education and religion were strong. Here, a Mrs Curry reigned supreme, charging a weekly fee of a penny or twopence to each pupil.

The Fell-em-Doon school was always the site of some activity. Every weekday winter evening, it played host either to the colliery band for practices or to a dancing class. On Sunday mornings a Sunday School was held there, while at six o'clock in the evening there would be a church service. In the fine weather this service was held outdoors among the heather.

The school survived until 1873 when the new Bothal National School was opened on 1 December of that year. It had its first inspection and examination on 24 February 1875. Night school began there on 2 October 1876, with 51 students on the roll. Seven years after its opening, there were 97 boys and 59 girls on the school register. Extensions were built, paid for by both the workmen and the coal owners.

Much later, in 1920, the Ashington Mining or Day Continuation School started. All Ashington Coal Company employees between the age of 16 and 18 were eligible to attend. Students had to undertake to complete the full course which lasted three years and entailed two full days' paid attendance per week as well as homework. There were also advanced classes in mining, electrical and mechanical engineering. It was possible for students to leave with their Managers' Tickets (They were

Bill Summers, mining student

qualified to become colliery managers.) My Uncle Jack Summers was among the first students to attend and later, my brother Bill continued his education there.

Hand in hand with the building of schools went the slow but steady march of religion which, like the colliery itself, was to provide a focus for so much of Ashington's community life. The first Wesleyan chapel was erected at High Market in 1876, a year after the foundation of the mechanics' institute and just at the start of the great period of educational expansion. Other churches, of various denomination, soon followed. In 1888, with the building of the Church of the Holy Sepulchre, Ashington became an ecclesiastical parish. A Presbyterian church was built in 1891, a Primitive Methodist one in 1892, the Salvation Army and a Christian Lay church in 1901 and a Catholic church in 1905. (In 1893 Father O'Hear came to Ashington and held the first Catholic Mass in the Co-op Hall).

Life, however, did have more to offer than working, learning and praying. Ashington, from its very beginning, had shown great ingenity in devising entertainments.

In 1865, Thomas A. Clarke got a few men together to play the first cricket match using the bat, ball and stumps he had made himself. In the same year the colliery owners bought a drum and twelve instruments so that the men might have a band. As soon as the instrumentalists were sufficiently proficient they learned a march and decided to put it to good use: they marched past the house of Mr Henderson, the owner. They were in some fear lest the length of the tune should fall short of the distance they had to travel! Happily, their fears were not realized.

The colliery band grew in number and ability till it was in demand and began to enter prize contests. The colliery owners gave the players every encouragement, often paying for new instruments.

As the band went from strength to strength, it soon needed professional teachers. Competition became keener and some-times good players were taken on at the colliery solely for their playing. They did token work down the pit and spent the rest of the time practising.

The great day for the band was Miners' Picnic Day. The

colliery band assembled as early as 6 am in the colliery yard. At the canteen the players were given a huge breakfast, after which they marched up and down the Rows playing. Men, women and children would fall in behind them and walk to the club where transport was waiting to take them to the picnic. At the club as many pints of beer as the bandsmen could drink were laid out for them in readiness.

Once at the picnic town they dismounted from their transport, got into lines, raised their banner and started playing and marching to the ground. On one occasion as Ashington Colliery Band walked through the gates a man shouted: 'You're the hundredth band through.'

After it was all over the bandsmen were offered hospitality from the various miners and their wives living in the area. This included a wash and brush-up (sometimes performed in the yard) and a splendid home-made tea. Afterwards, the visitors accompanied the man of the house to a working-men's club for the evening. Some of the younger men did not arrive back home till next day.

Another annual event was the Hospital Carnival Week, ending on the Saturday with Ashington *en fête*. The Main Street was thronged for the procession of the Beauty Queen and her retinue, children in fancy-dress, colliery carts and coal lorries cleaned up and adorned with tableaux of various sorts, beautifully groomed pit ponies being led by their drivers, the Woodhorn Knuts and the Coronation Jazz Band (both adult jazz bands) and the people with their collecting boxes.

In the park there were tents displaying the results of a plethora of competitions. The park was also the location for numerous mechanical races of the Wansbeck Motor Club, and night-time 'shows' made lively with naphtha flares, bright lights, shuggy boats, steam organs, favour sellers and all the noisy agglomeration that goes with the determination to have a good time and to be seen and heard to do so.

Thomas A. Clarke's first makeshift cricket venture turned out to be the harbinger of more elaborate sporting events. With so much of life lived underground or indoors, a chance for exercise in the open was always welcome. By 1886 the 'Rec' (recreation ground) was already in existence, offering cricket, wrestling, an annual sports day and bicycle racing. Some of these races lasted a whole day. In 1920 the coal company provided funds for a 'welfare department', which brought together educational, sporting and leisure-time activities. Its 60 acres of land became a regular venue for games of cricket, rugby, football and hockey.

Towards the end of the nineteenth century the Miners' Hall was built by the Miners' Lodge, and this broadened the field of entertainment. Before this time, 'Penny Readings' had been given on Saturday nights, when poems and stories were read to listeners who had paid a penny entrance! There were also 'Threepenny Gaffs' – plays given by strolling players. On occasion, there was also a performing bear.

Ashington and District Sunday Lecture Society was instituted in 1907 in the Miners' Theatre. During the evening musical selections were provided by the Ashington Harmonic Society's Orchestra Band under the baton of Tom Boutland. My grandfather was a scene shifter and curtain operator here in his spare time. He seems to have been the senior man because he was paid 1s 6d. (7½p) per night while the others were paid a shilling (5p).

At the Miners' Theatre in the early days, there was a pantomime at Christmas. For the rest, there was drama performed by groups of travelling players. These were also the early days of the cinematograph, then called the 'living pictures' or, on the posters, the 'Bioscope'. Because of theatrical commitments, it was only on rare occasions that the hall could host a full week's booking.

Sunday evening shows became popular but they did not start till 7.45pm, so as not to interfere with church services. The cinematograph had no permanent housing and was placed upon a trestled table at the back of the theatre and seats were roped off to keep the audience away from the machinery.

On one occasion an enterprising company booked the theatre for two consecutive Sundays. They had a packed and appreciative audience. The first film was a French comedy about a dog of doubtful pedigree who mistook a butcher's shop for a prototype canine self-service. This was followed by an awe-inspiring film

Miners' theatre, Ashington

about the rugged scenery of Norway with its rushing torrents, craggy snow-capped heights and picturesque inhabitants. No detail of Norway was left unchronicled and the picture stretched to an interminable length.

The following Sunday there was again a capacity audience. Again, the little dog of the obscure pedigree, the frenzied butcher, the exasperated gendarmes and the motley throng. Again, the panorama of Norway. For a while there was silence then came the solitary, low whistle which was quickly multiplied and amplified and supported by boos and stamping feet and shouts of 'Tyek if off. Tyek it off.'

The operator stopped the film and addressed the audience in pained terms. 'Ladies and gentlemen,' he said, 'we are endeavouring to show you part of Scandinavia. I am astonished at this inexplicable and unseemly outburst. Why this shameful conduct? There are many among you who, in these dark winter mornings will descend the mine and not return till darkness has again descended. Tonight we give you an opportunity to see the Land of the Midnight Sun. We are trying to give you a modicum of knowledge regarding other lands. How many among you have little children at home? What happier picture can there be than these little children kneeling at their mother's knee and listening to stories of other lands? Travel broadens the mind. This film is of great educational value. It may even inspire younger minds with a spirit of adventure. Where would we be without these dauntless mountaineers of indomitable spirit? I hope the programme will be allowed to proceed with the utmost decorum and without further interruption.'

The malcontents (the majority) were stunned into silence by this rhetoric and no further sound was heard as the operator turned the handle at a uniformly ponderous speed – a brave undertaking considering the proximity of the stalls (then called 'the chairs'). It is questionable who was the more relieved, he or the audience, when the pianist burst into the National Anthem.

Later, Friday nights were known as 'Gozy' nights, evenings of 'Go as You Please' where anyone who felt he or she had talent could elect to perform. The question then was, 'Are ye gan t' the Gozy?'

The theatre also booked variety shows, where any jokes about the Labour Party were met with a very frosty and silent reception.

New debating and literary societies, home-grown concerts, amateur theatricals and operas flourished, continuing even after the talking pictures arrived.

For me as a child, though, my most vivid memories are of those outings that long practice had made almost traditional. At Easter most people went to Sheepwash ('Shiprish') to 'bool thor eggs'. Complete with baskets containing bread and butter and something to drink, they found a spot on the bank down which to roll coloured 'pace eggs' to see how far they would go without disintegrating. Also, eggs were 'jarped' – that is, their strength was tested against the strength of an opponent's egg. The egg was held firmly in one hand, the top showing. The opponent 'jarped' it by bringing his egg down in an effort to break the other. The winner was then 'jarped' in turn until one egg was proved strongest.

The remains of the eggs were eaten with the bread and butter. The repast often included bits of soil and grass still sticking to the eggs that hadn't emerged from the afternoon's exercises unscathed. This Easter fare was washed down with water, tea, lemonade or a concoction of liquorice dissolved in water. After that there was time to 'dee yor dickers', (act themselves) 'coupin' creels',(somersault) 'coppin' flooks wi' pins fer yucks', (fishing with a bent pin) playing 'moont the cuddy', (a sort of leap frog) and swinging on trees. The air was full of laughter and shrieks of fun.

The sea at Newbiggin, Cresswell or Druridge was only a tidy walk away. Here, the sand was always warm and golden (or so it seems now) and there was enough water for everyone to plodge in comfort. Willicks (winkles) were to be found in quantity on the rocks, though collecting them was often painful. The small pieces of rock and pebbles were sharp and hurtful to bare feet. The willicks were collected in pails, boiled and the cooked delicacy poked out with a pin and eaten. Everyone remarked on how tasty they were, but I did not like them and thus I felt rather cheated in not being able to enjoy something that everyone liked so much.

On the grass skirting the dunes men were often to be seen playing 'pot-share bools' (bowls). Those taking part played in their underwear – linings (long johns) and body shirt (vest). The course was usually three miles long and each competitor took a ball and threw it underarm as far as he could, the object being to cover the course in as few throws as possible. Behind the men walked their supporters laying bets.

In the spring a trip to the bluebell woods at Bothal was a must. There they were, underneath the trees, making a carpet of such an incredible blue as to make both sea and sky, pale into

Dressed for potshare bowling

insignificance. Unfortunately, the way through the woods was often strewn with wilting bluebells which had been picked and later discarded.

The countryside immediately adjacent to the pit was marred by the covering of fine coal dust that was its inevitable heritage. Further out, however, the country flourished as it always had done and here were the 'walks' without which, for the majority of the population, no Sunday would have been complete.

The mothers' and fathers' walk started from High Market, up to Cooper's Shop. (A bitter disappointment to me, this: it wasn't a proper shop, merely called so because barrels had once been made here.) From here they'd go left to the Dene, left again and up to Herdman's Farm. For most of its length the walk was level and, therefore, suitable for pram-pushing or for young legs. The walk could, of course, be done in reverse. Thus one met the majority of one's neighbours, friends and relatives. It was difficult indeed not to stop to chat with particular people for one reason or another. By the time we reached Herdman's Farm we had invariably collected either a posse of relatives or those workmates of my father who were keen gardeners. Thus the walk ended with our going to the allotments. Here we first of all walked up and down slowly while my parents pointed out the success (or, rarely, failure) of one crop of vegetables and fruit after another (rhubarb, red and black currants, gooseberries, beetroot, marrows, leeks, lettuce, chives, onions, shallots, cauliflowers, parsnips, broccoli, Brussels sprouts, sage, parsley, runner beans, broad beans, peas, turnips, spring cabbages, cabbages, savoys, celery . . .). Then came a discourse on the relative merits of the noble potato – Duke of York, Queen Mary, Edgills Blue, Up to Date, Alley, Great Scott, Aaron Chief, Kerrs Pink, Midlothian, D. Vernon, Warwick Castle, King Edward and Roderick Dew – and the yield that could be expected from any one shaw of these potatoes.

It was a trying time for us children. We could not run about because of any possible damage to our Sunday clothes, and, after our allotment had been reviewed, we then had to spend a comparable amount of time in the allotments of the people who had admired ours.

For married couples still active and unencumbered by children, there was usually a choice of two walks. Instead of turning off to go to the Dene, they could carry on to Sheepwash and walk along by the river Wansbeck, climbing the bank to Herdman's Farm, or they could walk to Bothal by the road and come back through the fields. The walk through the fields to Longhirst and back was, for some reason, reserved for courting couples who had pledged their troth and were about to tie the knot.

All of these walks took place in spring, summer, early autumn and winter afternoons. On winter nights Bothal Bank was the haunt of the middle-teens (although the word had not then been coined). It was blacker than midnight because of the proliferation of over-hanging trees. The boys lined the railings of the bank as it snaked its way steeply to the bottom. The girls walked past in twos and threes for protection. Without warning, an arm would shoot out and a high squeal of horrified delight would break on the not-so-silent air. Then there was great conjecture as to who it was. Some well-to-do lads had flashlights which they suddenly switched on in the faces of the approaching girls. If, alas, the beam revealed a wallflower the torch would be switched off quickly (it wasn't worth wasting the battery) and there would follow a disgruntled, 'Aw. It's ony hor from . . .' And so the girls concerned would have an unmolested passage down the bank. When that happened, the only thing to do was to go back up to the top and come down again and try your luck a second time. If the light was flashed on someone of fairer mien it was kept there while the damsel so caught struggled to get out of the limelight screaming, 'Purrit off. Stop it.' This maiden and her cohorts were then assured of being pushed and jostled down the length of the bank.

This, then, was Ashington, young, vibrant with life and growing. Its main street stretched for over two miles from Ellington Road Ends to the Grand Corner, where it dissolved into Woodhorn and Hirst. It was recognized as the largest mining village in the world.

2. Church and School

For the first five years of my life, the hub of the largest mining village in the world was 180 Station Road, a bottom flat at the bottom end of Ashington: there, I was born.

I was a sickly child and, because of a recurring illness, I spent a great deal of my time in a bed placed against the window so that I might get a view of the front street. I came to know this view very well.

The flat was situated near the bar of a T-junction. Immediately

to the left of our front door was another front door and, next to that, a fish and chip shop. Next to the fish and chip shop was the Church Hall (or Parish Hall, as it was usually called) and, in the same building, the houses of the sexton and the curate. I could not see these buildings from my window but I was aware of their existence from my earliest days.

The Parish Hall was where the Mother's Union, Scouts, Guides, Cubs, Brownies, the Sale of Work people – indeed, any group or society connected with the church – met. Here also the choir tea, all church socials, including the Harvest Social and Sunday School parties, took place.

It was here that I made my stage début. Bothal schools gave a concert. I do not know exactly what the programme entailed: I can only remember three incidents. The first was when we were allowed to look at the Fairy Queen all dressed in white with gauzy white wings. This was Marjorie Brotherton. I thought she was the most beautiful thing I'd ever seen and I longed to be chosen, one day, to be a Fairy Queen myself – one of my many unfulfilled ambitions.

I was among the chorus line that opened the evening's performance. I had happily endured a sleepless night because my hair was tortured into curl rags. My big moment arrived when I was one of a line of little girls all dressed in white with large blue bows of ribbon in our hair. With a little help from the piano we sang, with appropriate actions:

Oh Good Evening,
Pray how do you do?
We are babies
Come to sing to you.
Cheeks like roses,
Hair that's all acurl,
How d'you like to be a Baby Girl?

When the Bogey
Man comes in at night,
Eyes like saucers
Giving you a fright,
You must run to Mummy.
She will put it right
How d'ye like to be a Baby Girl?

The next item was a playlet especially for the little boys. They were dressed as chickens. That is, they wore their Sunday trousers, white cricket shirts and yellow paper hats with beaks made to look like chickens. In their careful rehearsals, no one had prepared them for the burst of applause that greeted them. Also in the rehearsals, the 'chickens' had picked up pretend corn scattered by the big lad (from the top infants) in charge. To give verisimilitude to the action on the night, pretend corn was replaced by dolly mixtures. Put off by the applause, the boys had to be prompted into action by the teacher in the wings (Miss Anderson). The eye of Authority temporarily taken off him, the lad with the dolly mixtures – an opportunist – crammed as many as he could into his mouth and had difficulty with his line, 'Here chicky-chicks.' Also there was less corn to scatter. When the 'chickens' saw the dolly mixtures rolling about the stage, they could hardly believe their eyes for a second, but only for a second. The play forgotten, it was every 'chicken' for himself. Inevitably, some got more than others. All in all, these were two difficult acts to follow.

As a child, for me the highlight of the Parish Hall year was the choir concert, directed and produced by the organist and choir master, Mr George Turnbull.

The concert began with new musical items from the whole choir, practised in honour of the occasion. I was anxious for these to be over: it was the items they did every year that I waited for. There were some excellent singers in the choir. The lead boy soprano, Ernie Hamilton, always sang 'Oh, for the Wings of a Dove' and then, later on, 'Hear my Prayer'. There was a duet sung by Mr and Mrs Turnbull and at least two items from the Gleemen, a quartet made up of George Turnbull, Richard Barnfather, Henner Wanless and Uncle Jack Summers. The first number was always serious and the second always called 'Women', the end of which was sung to actions and went like this:

> *There are women who are witty,*
> *There are women who are pretty,*
> *There are women who are very big and fat and RED* [Pause, laughter]
> *There are women who are sainted,*
> *There are women who are painted,*
> *There are women who don't GOSSIP* – [Pause]
> *But . . .* [Longer pause]
> *THEY'RE DEAD.* [Prolonged laughter and applause]

I almost fell off the form laughing. Almost. Once you were off, you didn't get back on again. People just thankfully gave themselves more room. We were 'fair scumfished'.

A group of the men the Gleemen did a number called 'Shall Ashington Have A Pump?' I cannot remember the lyrics. I don't think I ever heard it. I only waited for the glorious moment when Uncle Jack stood up – minus his dentures – weeping as he sang and mopping his eyes with a handkerchief already saturated with water. When he squeezed it out, the water cascaded on to the table round which the Gleemen sat and tears of laughter cascaded down my cheeks as I watched.

My father always did a solo item when he dressed up and sang a Tyneside song, usually 'The Row Upon the Stairs' or 'The Nibors Doon Bela'. He interspersed the verses with 'patter' he'd written himself. I thought it was hilarious. The concert finished with the Gleemen coming on as Eastern maidens in yashmaks and gauzy costumes, their underwear, socks and suspenders showing through, or as ballet dancers with crêpe-paper skirts, skimpy tops, flowers in their hair and, of course, the inevitable socks and suspenders. Then they did an appropriate dance. My side ached by the time we stood up, straightened ourselves out and sang the National Anthem.

On the bar of the T-junction stood the Church of the Holy Sepulchre, Church of England. I was familiar with this building also from my earliest days. All my father's family were Church of England. That I always recognized one could worship at another denomination lay in the fact that, just as I always knew Ashington, so I knew Wooler from which my mother came. My mother's family were Presbyterians and when we holidayed in Wooler we attended that church.

The vicar at Ashington, the Reverend Samuel Davidson, was elderly when I first became aware of him. He was a tall, well-made man whose cassock and surplice made him look even bigger. He had grey hair and curls that clung to his head. Bushy grey eyebrows shielded his eyes, so that you never knew whether they were open or shut. He looked very like what I imagined God to be. It was obvious that he and God were very intimate because he had an extremely confidential delivery, so confidential that it seemed like eavesdropping to listen to him during the service. And what he and God talked about pleased him because there was always a benign smile lurking round his lips, for ever anxious to come quietly to the surface. In his early, youthful days he had been an athlete (a 'Blue', we were told) and he had frequently played football in a nearby field with young miners 'tekkin his jacket off just like anybody else an' playin' in his dog-collar'.

The minister at Wooler was different. He had a dramatic delivery that had the congregation sitting up smartly in their seats paying attention. His eyes swept the devout, constantly alert, and his finger admonished or emphasized as occasion demanded: 'And GORD shall whipe eway orl tearce from their eyce.'

Every fourth Sunday in Ashington we had Sunday School in church during which time the vicar gave a little homily to us children. There was no need for him to keep his eyes on us as he spoke. If zeal for his subject brought him among us in the body of the church, it was in an effort to get his point across or draw nearer to God, not to see whether or not we were attending. His wife, Mrs Davidson, did that with commendable efficiency from the back of the church. Any fidgeters were given a poke in the back with her forefinger, or with the point of her umbrella if the culprits were further away. The sensation was the same. A modest cough was enough to acquaint the Sunday School teachers that one of their number had a pupil not attending. A look was all that was needed. A second cough meant that the offender was 'brought to the back', the ultimate disgrace.

On the other three Sundays we went to Bothal schools to recite the catechism in our various classes. We did this in a chant similar to the one we used on weekdays to recite tables or poetry – 'Once eight is eight . . .' 'My Godfathers and godmothers . . .' 'I wandered lonely as a cloud . . .'

The Wooler Sunday School was held in the morning and here we were told Biblical stories. School ended with our going into church to sing a children's hymn and then to walk out importantly before the sermon. The 'country children' were allowed to wait for their parents in the vestry where they could read quietly.

My grandmother had her own pew in this church with her name on it, MRS MARGARET GALLON. When we attended the services proper, we went there.

The seats in Ashington church were polished forms with backs to them, and bare wooden forms to kneel on for prayers. There were no names on the seats but all my family had their own favourite rows.

Knowing that it was possible to worship equally at two churches, by the time I was ten I had sampled what else was on offer, ecclesiastically speaking, in Ashington.

The Presbyterian church was smaller and more compact than the Church of England church. The pews were of polished dark oak as was the pulpit and the table beneath on either side of which were the chairs for the choir. The whole appeared warm and cosy; a blend of red plush and rich wood. The Sunday School was held in the room adjacent. Here, we got a card with stars for attendance-marks and, often, a short piece of text in the shape of a cross or set on an ornate card bordered in multi-coloured flowers.

There was a Sunday School Christmas party and the Sunday School trip which travelled a little farther afield than did the Church of England trip at that time. At the former, we travelled by train to Whitley Bay; at the latter we travelled in cleaned-out colliery farm carts to Cresswell.

At the end of the year we got medals and books for good attendance. These were presented at the anniversary, that is, the anniversary of the founding of the Sunday School. A fête day.

An odd little incident happened about this time. I had heard of the Lido Lady, a young avant-garde Miss whose reputed lifestyle was equal to anything the *News of the World* could conjure up. 'She has more massacre on them eyes than I have black lead on me grate,' one incensed matron said of her. It appeared that while other right-minded people went to church on Sunday mornings, or stayed at home to make the dinner, the Lido Lady habituated one of the ice-cream shops. One Monday morning a friend of mine was able to boast she had actually seen her and talked to her the previous morning. She had gone into the ice-cream shop, ordered a penny mug of Oxo and had spoken to the Lido Lady (all dressed in red) while she sipped her nectar.

Next Sunday I decided on a desperate plan. I would set off for church *but I would not go*. Instead, I would visit the ice-cream shop and spend my collection penny on a mug of Oxo that I too might talk with this exalted being. As I walked past the church, my collection clutched in my sweating palm, my footsteps faltered. I was 200 per cent sure to be found out. Within minutes of the service being over, news of my absence would somehow reach our house. And, worse than my non-attendance would be the crime that I had spent the collection earmarked for some mission of good intent. To bolster my flagging courage, I devised a plan. I would count to ten and try the first shop doorway I came across. If it was locked, I would go on; if the shop was open, I would spend half of my collection, thus giving way to at least semi-wickedness, and go to church and put only a halfpenny on the plate. As all the shops (except the ice-cream shop) on the main street were closed on a Sunday, the result was a foregone conclusion, but at least it took the immediate burden of my projected misdeeds from my shoulders and placed it on those of Chance.

The shop I chose was a small greengrocery-cum-sweet-cum-general dealers (whose name I have forgotten) next to Gardiner's the Baker's. The blinds were down. All was silence. I tried the door. It opened!! Hardly able to believe what had happened, I went cautiously into the shop. It was in semi-darkness. I took a few uncertain steps forward. Everwhere the blank, lifeless, dispirited, silent, almost ghostly air. I called, 'Shop' feebly – and suffered the same fate as the 'Traveller'. No one answered. I rapped on the counter with my penny. No one came. I went outside. The police station wasn't far away but I didn't have to go there. In the nearly deserted street, two policemen were approaching with measured tread.

'Please,' I said, 'that shop door's open and there's nobody in. I think they've forgotten to lock the door.'

They went back in with me and scoured the shop. No one there. One of the policemen went to fetch the owner. She returned with him in a short while, terribly shaken because of the 'pollis' having come to the house and the thought of the shop's standing open and what might have happened.

'Check if anything's missing,' one policeman said.

She was hardly capable of doing that, so great was her agitation but finally they were convinced nothing had been taken.

'You've been lucky,' they said, and she could only nod in agreement. We stood outside while, still in a shake she locked the door and went off padding away in her bedroom slippers.

'You've been a good girl,' the policemen said to me in approval. 'Where were you going?' Basking in this approval, how could I tell them of my fell purpose?

'To church,' I said.

'You're a bit late,' one observed, looking at the council clock. 'But we'll see that they let you in.'

The Elder opened the door gingerly so that he made no noise. the more gently he pushed it, the more the door squeaked and screeched in protest.

'Sit at the back,' he whispered, so that everybody in the last four rows turned round to see what was happening.

I sat down marvelling. God had gone to an awful lot of trouble to see that one eight-year-old lamb did not stray from the fold and the missionaries got their penny.

The Methodists also gave ornate texts as an inducement to attend Sunday School every week. They had *viva voce* examinations which counted towards attendance when it came to the annual prize-giving. As the child nominated to take the collection went round we sang:

> *Hear the pennies dropping,*
> *Listen while they fall,*
> *Every one for Jesus*
> *He has made them all.*

They were more overt about their anniversary: all and sundry were invited. On the morning of the anniversary, the Sunday School superintendent took his charges to selected Rows to give a preview of the afternoon's celebration. They had with them a harmonium on a hand cart. One of the Sunday School teachers played the instrument while the scholars sang a hymn, then the superintendent gave a cordial invitation to everyone, requesting the pleasure of their company at the anniversary. A little girl in her best dress would be stood on the hand cart to recite:

> *I cannot say a very long piece,*
> *Because I am so small.*
> *I've just come along to tell you,*
> *Jesus loves you all.*

At the Salvation Army, Sunday clothes weren't so important. Nor was the collection. What really mattered was, could you go round with a collecting box getting other people to contribute?

The Salvation Army held more meetings in the open air than they did in their barracks, especially in the summer. During the week they held meetings on most evenings somewhere in the Rows. By the time they'd got into a circle and played one verse of 'Beulah Land', a fair crowd of children and adults would be in evidence. The children came nearer the Salvationists than did the adults, who stayed within the boundaries of their own dwellings or those of their neighbours, either leaning on the fence or on the bottom half of the stable door if they had a back-end.

The hymn ended, a man (rarely a woman) usually stood up to give his testimony – to speak of his wild, dissipated younger days before he had seen the light and had been saved. He pleaded with his listeners to reflect on their sins and to consult the Good Book before it was too late. Then the captain spoke of the joy it had brought to them all to see the soul of their dear brother saved and if any other dear brother or dear sister listening wished to join their happy band they had only to come to the barracks at any time. After another stirring hymn they got ready to march down the Row to another meeting-place, their banner of blood and fire borne aloft by the standard-bearer and the band following behind playing 'Stand Up, Stand Up for Jesus'. The Salvationists with their tambourines and money boxes moved hopefully forward as one by one the adults melted into their homes before the box got to them.

At weekends they were a fixture at the Grand Corner on Saturday nights. They stood around with their flag spread on the ground, played hymns, spoke and encouraged those listening to throw coppers on to the flag.

It took a great deal of courage to enter the Roman Catholic church. I wasn't of their faith so I went there in fear and trembling, expecting to be thrown out any minute. Having got in, I was fascinated. I watched what others did and followed their actions, dipping in the holy water and genuflecting. The Stations of the Cross, the figures of Christ and the Virgin Mary held me entranced. It seemed much easier to pray there than at other churches. At least you could see what you were praying to.

Not only did I visit the churches, but I also attended their various youth organizations: the lantern lectures, the King's Messengers, the Sons and Daughters of Temperance, the Rechabites, the Band of Hope, the Sunbeams and the Brownies. For various reasons my name did not remain long on their books – indeed, sometimes I did not survive as a member beyond the initial 'free' meetings.

In general, the churches supplied a plethora of activities apart from those I've already mentioned. There were, for instance, prayer meetings, Sisterhood, Pleasant Sunday Afternoons, Pleasant Sunday Evenings, men's societies, the Christian Endeavour, bazaars, Bible classes, Boys Brigades and lectures.

It was the churches, also that determined the dates for us to wear new clothes or change into winter or summer attire. Most people got something new for Easter. Whit Sunday was definitely the day for wearing new summer clothes or bringing out last year's 'summer best' (which had been carefully put away) regardless of the weather. Usually, Harvest Festival Sunday was the one on which we wore new winter clothes or released last year's 'winter best' from mothballs. Only Mrs Davidson, the vicar's wife, was, like Queen Mary, above fashion. She was very slim and wore a close-fitting, floor-length brown/snuff-coloured coat with slightly puffed sleeves, feather boa and very wide hat with restrained flowers smothered by a veil.

When I started the grammar school (or secondary school, as it was then called) I lost interest in the peripatetic religious life and returned to the Church of England, from which I then defected only once. This was when a group of evangelists came from America and held daily meetings in the Central Hall for a fortnight. The group consisted of a preacher, the Reverend H. Andrew Morrison, and a group of four black spiritual singers. I went with my friend Joyce Clark, and we were hooked from the beginning. So many people wanted to hear them that they gave two houses, as it were, and those who came to the first house were asked not to stay for the second. We attended the first house, but the plea not to stay on fell on deaf ears as far as we were concerned. We got up to go with the others, but dawdled and hung back so that we were among the first to be seated in the second house. My Aunt Martha, who was a staunch Methodist and a member of the Sisterhood, spoke to me gently and said we weren't being fair. It didn't make any difference.

I returned to the Church of England with the vague feeling that you went to church and made your contact with God in much the same way as you went to Bedlington Secondary instead of Morpeth High, or lived in your own house in preference to a colliery house, or lived in Ashington as opposed to Hirst.

(That I have actually written 'Hirst' is possibly attributable to Miss Polly Weatherley, a teacher at Bothal School. She waged an unceasing campaign to get children to say 'Hirst' instead of 'th' Horst'. The offending child would be brought to the front of the class and slapping the culprit's bottom to get her message home, Miss Weatherley would say, 'It is *"Hirst"* not *"the Hirst"*'. You do not say The Ashington or The Newbiggin, do you?'

'No, Miss,' tearfully.

'No, Miss What?' and a harder smack.

'No, Miss Weatherley.' But we went on saying 'th' Horst', just the same.)

I gained the idea that the Central Hall Methodists were the most enterprising and gave the best lantern lectures, but it was difficult to imagine you were in church at all here. The seats were wooden tip-up ones and there was no air of sanctity. The Salvation Army certainly seemed the most fun; the Primitive Methodists the most glum and humourless; and the Catholic Church the most awe-inspiring. The Presbyterian Church was, I felt, for the well read and well-heeled. I think it was the red carpets and the suggestion of plushness, and the most attractive Reverend F.P. Copeland Simmons, that combined to give me this impression.

The Church of England offered no inducements to its faithful. The seats were hard and uncovered and the forms on which we knelt to pray even harder and unyielding. There were hassocks hanging from little hooks under the seat in front that could be used, but I always felt this was an indulgence and something I must not give way to. I had already formed the impression that, to be efficacious, prayers had to be uttered under some discomfort, the more the better. My nightly prayers had to be said in a chill bedroom with me kneeling on glacial linoleum. Prayers said in comfort beneath flannelette sheets, blankets and quilts had no real effect.

Next to the church was a small cluster of trees called, locally, 'the plantin'. I suspect it was all that was left of the wooded, whin-covered area where the early Fell-em-Doonians met on warm summer evenings. It should have been a haven for children to play in, but I never saw this happen. Perhaps it was the nearness of the church and the churchyard which prevented them from doing so. It certainly could be an eerie place on a cold blustery night with a fitful moon, the wind soughing through the branches and moving the street lamp (the one lit by the lamplighter with his long pole), so that the pools of shadow shifted to intensify the darkness of the bulk of the church and the space beyond it which was filled with silent tombstones and the even more silent dead. You couldn't see them, but you knew they were there.

For those who did not use the plantin as a short-cut, it was necessary to walk round by the railings and pass a number of retired miners resting on seats built into a semi-circle of pavement which took up some of the plantin area. These miners would be 'tekkin' thor pipe' or 'hevin' a crack'. Incidentally, pipes were called clays. They could be bought for as little as a penny and sometimes a box of matches was 'thrown in'.

The railings curved to the left and following the curve you came to a sprinkling of working-men's clubs, houses and shops on the left and, on the right, the First Row, more houses and more shops. The First Row was where the colliery manager and sundry officials lived. The first houses were fairly big and the others rather smaller.

We lived in 'Dunedin' for a year or two. Of all the gardens we had, this was the one I liked most. It was mostly trees, lawn, path and rockery so that it required little more than an occasional brush with a lawn-mower. In autumn the ground was a glorious riot of colour when the leaves fell. The house itself was roomy and airy, containing on its ground floor an entrance hall, three reception rooms, an enormous kitchen, a scullery, a walk-in pantry and numerous cupboards. Upstairs we had a bathroom, a lavatory and four large bedrooms, the master bedroom having its own dressing-room. Outside, there were numerous outhouses, one of which was the inevitable wash-house, bigger than most and therefore more suitable for wash-house drama. Indeed, the first writing I ever did for public acclaim was a play to be performed in a friend's mother's wash-house. The pit, stalls and green room, together with the poss-barrel, mangle, set-pot and bench were housed in a theatre about three times the size of a telephone kiosk. In this space four Thespians played out the tragedy I had written while the audience of three (mothers) did their best to keep their faces straight. As was customary on these occasions we propped a bit of slate up against the window and scrawled on it, 'Play tonight. Two pins to get in'. Also, as was customary no-one paid. These new premises opened up hopes of a musical extravaganza.

Once Mr Jonathan Moberley Pumphrey (one of the mine owner's sons) left his bicycle unattended in our yard. He had bought it specifically for going to the pit. It was a lady's bike, a museum piece even then. It had come down in the world literally and figuratively, for it was spending its declining years in the sale room at the bottom of the rather steep flight of stairs on the station bank when he rescued it, paying 7s. 6d. (37½p) for the privilege. It was black, tall and stately, with most of the cords laced from the mudguard to the hub broken. It operated a back pedal brake.

But it was a bike. And, as I said, unattended.

I looked at it and wondered what it would be like to wheel it. There wasn't much scope in the yard. There was no one about. I took it out into the lane just to walk it to the corner and back. I couldn't reach the seat and I couldn't ride, but I just wondered what it would be like to sort of put my foot on the pedal and see if I could make it go. I managed a wobble. And then another. And, oh joy! When I kept the pedals going I could stay upright. I was riding! It was wonderful! But the end of the block loomed up and I couldn't stop and I might run into something and I didn't know what to do, so I turned the wheel to the end of the kerb and the bicycle swerved and I fell off with the bike on top of me – I'm glad to say.

I picked myself and the bike up, not in the least concerned about any damage I might have done to my person. I examined the bike. It seemed all right. The only thing was, a pedal had dropped off. I tried to screw it back in but the threads were worn. I wheeled the machine back to the yard and propped it up as I'd found it, shoving the pedal in place.

When next he rode the bike (at three in the morning) Mr Pumphrey either divined what had happened or an unseen witness had reported the whole incident to the right quarter.

'Tell Linda,' he said gently to my mother later, 'I don't mind her riding the bicycle, but she ought to have asked first. And she should have told me about the pedal. I wouldn't have been angry.'

When the parental aspect of this incident had been dealt with I presented myself to Mr Pumphrey at the first opportunity, my mouth dry, my bones turned to jelly and my blood to water as I apologized for what I had done and what had happened.

He smiled, nodded, and – gave me the bike! Coals of fire, indeed!

The bike was a somewhat tetchy old lady but I respected her dignity and her age. Even with the seat down to its lowest level it was a little too high for me; yet we persevered. I would not suffer her to have a false pedal and together we went to Wooler and back twice. Of course, because of her advanced years even the smallest incline was too much for her, so I walked a fair part of the way.

This part of Ashington was High Market, once called Ashington Market, a pale shadow of its former self. Once it had been the hub of activity, the centre of business and commerce in the old Fell-em-Doon. People from surrounding villages came to shop here. Now only a somewhat faded working-men's club presented a blank façade and the name 'Fell-em-Doon' in memory of bygone times.

This road finally led to Bothal schools, a squat, single-storey, red-brick building situated between the Third Row and the Long Row. When the school bell pealed forth its summons all those scholars converging on the building had to take to their heels and run. Naturally, the further away you were the harder

Bothal Schools

had to run. Kindly souls in the Third Row would come to the yard fence and encourage the laggards to great efforts.

'Run, hinny, run or ye'll get the belt,' which was only too true. The minute the bell stopped a girl from Standard X Seven stood at the girls' gate and took names. A boy from Standard X Seven performed a like service at the boys' gate. Late-comers then had to wait till the 'lines' went in when the gates were locked.

Except in the most inclement weather – absolutely drenching rain or blinding snow – the entire population of the three schools, the Little School (infants') and the two Big Schools (boys' and girls') stood in lines in their respective yards, the class teachers at the head. When all lines were utterly still and perfectly straight, the teacher on duty in the various yards blew a whistle and the lines went in. My father told me that in his day, the boys in X Seven were allowed to whistle a marching tune as they went in. No such diversion was allowed to us, whatever standard we were in. The girls of X Seven stood at one end of the yard and, naturally, they went in first and were followed by the girls of Standard Seven. X Seven and Standard Seven were housed in the same classroom at the back of which stood the desk belonging to the head, Miss Dixon. Even with two classes, this room was less full then any other because some girls left without ever reaching Standard Seven. Next followed Standard Two,

Standard One, Standard Five and Standard Six. All these classes went in at the 'top end' of the school. All, including both Sevens, had to walk through the porch where hats and coats were hung, 'on the march'. The classroom next to the porch was Standard Six. A door led to Standards Two and One, Two being farthest away. The two classes were separated by a curtain. The class adjacent Standard Six was Standard Five. These classes were also separated by a curtain. Only Standards Five, Six and Seven were allowed to hang their coats in the first porch. Standards One and Two had to use the porch adjacent to Standard Two.

As these classes walked off the yard into the top doorway, Standards Four, Three and Three B (sometimes known as 'the Dunces') walked into school via the bottom door. Here, again, they had to go through a square porch, the largest in the girls' school. Standard Three walked in first, then Four and, lastly, Three B.

When the school was in, the late-comers were confronted by the teacher on duty. Most often she had her strap in her hand. This served to inhibit invention or a long-winded, heart-stirring explanation. If the first girl said, 'Aa slept the caallor,' all the others did, and they put out their hands automatically.

(This excuse was a throwback to some years before when a man – or woman – would go round knocking on doors calling the men up for the first shift, i.e. they were 'in forst'. If the caller knocked a pit-man up and he went back to sleep again, he had 'slept the caller'. This happened to my father when he was a young lad of 13. He had, by this time, been at the pit for over a year and was no longer a trapper lad, that is, he no longer had to sit by himself in the darkness in the trapper's hole opening and shutting the trap door that closed off the road leading to the face. He would have had a piece of stout string attached to the door and this he would have pulled when he heard the pit ponies and tubs approaching. The door would then open to let them through. Now, at 13, he worked on the tubs 'hingin' on and knockin' off'. In other words, he clipped and unclipped the tubs to and from the haulage rope. The house he lived in was very near that of the 'caallor' and so he was the first to be knocked up. He got ready for the pit but it was still much too early, so he sat down on the form next to the kitchen table and waited till he heard the footsteps of the men on their way to work. And there my grandmother found him fast asleep some three hours later.)

When it was Miss Weatherley's turn to admonish the tardy, she took the opportunity to continue her unrelenting crusade for correct speech.

'Why are you late?'

'Please, Miss. Aa slept the caallor.' Sniff.

'Please, Miss What?'

Sniff. 'Please, Miss . . . Miss Weatherley.'

'Now, why are you late? And *stop sniffing*, girl.'

'Please, Miss – Miss Weatherley – I slept the caallor.'

'The *what*?'

'The caallor. Please, Miss . . . Miss Weatherley.'

'You mean, you *overslept*,' with appropriate rein forcement.

'Yes, Miss. Please, Miss . . . Miss Weatherley.'

But we went on 'sleeping the caallor' just the same.

It was at Bothal scools that I began my formal education. An erratic attender, I spoiled the registers of Miss Wate, Miss Anderson, Mrs Storey, Mrs Duncan, Mrs Dodds, Miss Weatherley, Miss Crombie, Miss Weatherley (alas, she had to put up with me twice – Standard Four and Standard Six) and Miss Joisce.

I can remember only my first day in the infants' class where I survived only a few days. I spent a longer time in the next class with Miss Wate – dear, kind Miss Wate – for whom I had such a regard that I insisted on having my new dress made exactly like hers. Brown serge with heavy beaded embroidery probably looked well on her; on a thin waif, it was like a suit of armour.

Miss Anderson had a heavier responsibility than the other teachers in the Little School. She presided over the Top Infants. Her task was to prepare pupils for the Big School and the disposition of her class was after the Big School fashion. Each Friday, the class had a test carrying a total of 25 marks. By the end of the afternoon she had the results and those who had to move up or down did so. The 'A' section was housed in a vertical row of desks with backs to them and geared to hold two children each. They were placed on the right side of the room facing the teacher. The 'C' section on the opposite side of the class had desks capable of accommodating the same number of children, but there the similarity ended. The two back rows might contain their full quota of pupils, but the front row contained but a single child. This was so that Miss Anderson had somewhere other than the porch to put those children who misbehaved.

The 'B' section sat on forms at desks with long rigid tops and underneath long rigid shelves. There were no backs to these desks. You used the desk behind to lean against (if you dared) or the wall if you were in the back row. However, when you were neither writing, nor doing sums, nor working with plasticine, nor threading cards, you were sitting up straight with your hands behind your back. These 'B' desks were useful in that they could be made to accommodate the number required.

Slates and slate pencils were used and it was mandatory that each child brought a bottle of water and a slate rag to keep his or her slate clean. Spitting on the slate was expressly forbidden, as was rubbing it clean with an all-purpose jersey sleeve – yet there were one or two who did just that, employing their own spit and their jersey sleeves to clean their slates. (A description of such a sleeve is better left to the imagination.)

Friday after the mid-afternoon break was the time devoted to silent reading. During this time the teacher 'did' her register. Most teachers took great pride in their registers, which were very neat indeed with their slanting uniform strokes in blue and uniform circles penned in blue or red. A week with no one absent and no one late meant the class could 'get out soon' on Friday afternoon.

Thus it was that a class with me in it was handicapped. But I was not the only culprit. There were, among the girls, those who were kept off every Monday to help with the washing and those who stayed off every Friday to help with the cleaning, for, every Friday, each house had a mini spring-clean. Actually, most teachers were sympathetic, both to my absences and to those of the girls I've just mentioned. Regarding non-attendance, a School Board Man kept us all on our toes, parents included. And so closely knit was the neighbourhood, that anyone meeting a child of school age walking abroad during school hours felt entitled to ask him or her why he or she was not at school.

School Board inspectors and police on the look-out for truants were called 'school tooters'. One such man discovered a truant who ran away before he could be identified. Fleet of foot, the truant ran 'doon the Raas', the 'pollis eftor him', saw his own back door, rushed into the house and 'lowped' into bed beside his father who was on night shift.

Usually, every child could be identified and there was no need to ask his or her name. Surnames were hardly ever used. Nicknames were often passed on from one generation to the next. Thus, 'three toots t' Linton' (a tankey driver so called because when he and his mate approached the place where the lines diverged he would say, 'Now divvent ferget, it's three toots t' Linton') might well pass his name on to his son, though the latter never went anywhere near a tankey. (Tankeys were very small engines used mostly for taking pitmen to and from the outlying collieries. Miners' families could use them also. Those who did prudently took a paper to sit on.) 'Cakey' when he had a son became 'Owld Cakey' and his son 'Young Cakey'. When there was no nickname, the rhetorical question would be put to the school absentee: 'You're a Bell, aren't ye? Owld Tom's Lizzie's Young Lizzie's Little Lizzie?'

Often girls got up early on Monday morning to help their mothers with the washing before school. (Sometimes young lads also had to get up early to fill the set pot – a huge iron receptacle with a wooden lid set in a brick surround and having a fire underneath – before they went to school). Occasionally, too, a girl would ask permission to bring a younger sibling of two or three years of age to school with her. Probably this was to allow her mother to 'get on' or because her mother was 'off the crooks' (i.e. not very well). As the alternative was that the girl would have to stay at home, such permission was almost always given. The condition was, of course, that the child behaved. It was a privilege usually given because it was never abused.

The entire school was completely functional, every inch of space being in use all the time. Light came in from the tall narrow windows which were kept open at the top summer and winter alike. Heating was provided by a huge heavy black radiator – usually one per classroom – and any additional heat supplied by the thick heavy pipes connecting radiator with radiator. Regardless of weather and temperature, the central heating went on at a certain date and was switched off at a certain date. In extremely cold weather outdoor coats might be allowed in the classroom, but this was rare. The original oil-lamps still hung from the ceilings.

Other than the desks, the pattern and placing of which differed little from room to room, and the teacher's table or desk, the rooms contained a cupboard for books, needlework and craft materials and a large basket, similar to a laundry basket, which contained that class's stock of 'silent readers'. Standard Six had a piano. For singing lessons the curtain was drawn back and Standard Five and Six crowded together. I cannot recall whether or not other classes had a piano. I have a feeling they relied on a tuning fork and the ability of the class teacher to sing.

In Standard One we made sewing bags, large envelopes, all hemmed by hand and embroidered with a large cross-stitch around the border. We sat at our desks and the teacher walked round the classes, assessing and advising. She took the work home and examined the day's offerings. If the hemming had to be taken out, she inserted a pin marking off the point to which the unacceptable stitches had to be removed. The hem of my bag got progressively greyer with each passing week. When the bag was finished we had to bring material for a handkerchief. My mother, assessing accurately my lack of skill with a needle, gave me a piece of twill sheeting. It would have been almost as easy to sew a mail bag. Mrs Storey looked at the results of my struggles and said, 'I hope you never have a cold, Linda.'

The only garment I actually finished satisfactorily was a dress I made in Standard Four. (A pair of pink knickers attempted earlier had, unaccountably, a depth of two inches at the front and six at the back and one leg three inches longer and four inches wider than the other. Not even Mrs Dodds could figure out how I'd achieved this state of affairs.) I had arrived in Standard Four when all the others were well on and after many tears and much 'taking out', I asked if I might take my dress home to 'catch up'. That it arrived back the next week completely finished except for six inches of hem still to be sewn was accepted without comment.

In the Big School, slates were done away with, and in Standard One we began 'real writing'. First, we were given a pen shank, then a nib. We were instructed in the correct placing of the nib in the holder and given a dissertation on the use and care of a nib and the penalties visited on those whose nibs were forced into premature retirement through maltreatment. Next, we practised the use of the complete pen – without ink; how to dip the pen into the, as yet, empty inkwell, the pressure required to give the best results when the nib was applied to paper – thin strokes up, thick strokes down – how to hold the pen, how to sit when writing and how to rest the pen on the ledge. There was also instruction on the use and legitimate purpose of blotting paper. Slate monitors were now replaced by pen monitors and ink monitors, this last a most responsible position.

A great deal of care and character assessment, together with a knowledge of home circumstances, went into the selection of an ink monitor. The job was no sinecure. First of all, ink was made in school, to start with usually by the teacher but afterwards by the ink monitor. A sufficient quantity of ink was made on Monday mornings before school and inkwells had to be filled from the ink can by the monitor. Just the right amount had to be carefully poured in without spilling a drop, and throughout the week the inkwells had to be constantly checked. On Thursdays this was a tricky job. The monitor had to estimate that the fluid remaining would be equal to two days' work. On Friday afternoons the inkwells had to be washed ready for Monday. Thus the ink monitor had to be someone who could be relied upon to come to school early every morning without fail, who could be trusted on her own in the porch with ink powder and the mixed navy-blue liquid (of excellent staining properties) and who, on Friday afternoons could cleanse a number of small china inkwells without reducing their number and without diverting them to other uses. Even the most adept monitor could hardly avoid ink-strained hands or a smudge of navy blue somewhere on her person. A girl with a mother known to be especially particular about dress was out.

New nibs and fresh pieces of blotting paper were in the niggardly gift of teacher, who kept an accurate record of when the last nib or clean piece of blotting paper had been issued. Nor were replacements given out without evidence. The faulty nib or used blotting paper had to be inspected to ensure that there was no possibility of its being of further service. The same standards were applied to exhausted exercise books. There had to be no empty spaces and no sign of pages having been torn out. The penalty for this latter vandalism was dire.

Also, it was in Standard One that we learned to knit on short, thick wooden needles with pulled-out balls of wool. In no time at all, my 'knitting' was so tight that it was impossible to insert the right-hand needle into the loop for the first step of the operation 'in, over, through, out'.

The porches had uses other than being somewhere to put outdoor clothes. Here, the school 'norse' came on her ceaseless quest for nits. The senior girls' porch, being but a narrow corridor, was useless for this purpose so the girls of Standards Five, Six and Seven had their nits searched for in the space at the back of Standard Seven where Miss Dixon also held sway. Here we queued up in a silent, orderly fashion while the nurse's firm hands laid siege to our heads. The assistant handed out cards to those who harboured any unwelcome visitors and they were sent home with instructions. Mercifully, I never got a card. While I was at school my head was rigorously and firmly combed with a fine-tooth comb by my mother twice a week. As a result, my scalp was always tender to the touch. My hair was combed over a tray so that anything untoward was immediately identified. I still have that tray, just as I still have the amber medicine glass from which, every Friday night, my brother and I drank a vile concoction of Gregory powder in the interest of our bowels. I keep them as a reminder that there are some things I no longer have to endure.

Medical examinations were also held in the porches. Sometimes these examinations were extraneous to the routine ones. Many people were still, in the late 1920s and early 1930s, suffering from the effects of the 1926 strike. Medical examinations were given to determine undernourished children in need of a strength-building-up holiday.

Also during this time, benefactors came round with boots. They would go round, class by class, accompanied by Miss Dixon who was well aware of the circumstances of most of her pupils. Sometimes isolated children would be asked to come to the front, but most often it was virtually the whole class. Those who had to come out went up to the visitors, who were interested only in footwear. The girls had to turn the soles of their shoes up. Some children wore sandshoes summer and winter. Those who were poorly shod went to the porch where other people were waiting with large quantities of strong black boots. The girls came back to the class somewhat self-consciously in unbending, squeaky stout black-leather boots.

Most girls spent a year in each class. A few spent longer and another small group spent less – sometimes as little as one term. They moved up as soon as they'd finished the quota of work to be learned in that particular class. The core subjects were English exercises, composition, arithmetic, tables, spelling, reading and writing. Weekly examinations were held and the class shuffled round to new places. In spite of absences, I did not lose out because I read a great deal at home – not only my own books over and over again and those of my brother, but, nothing else being available, bits of *Harmsworth's Encyclopedia* and the conversation bits in Dickens and other classics. My father and mother both heard me spell regularly and kept me abreast of the 'times tables' and weights and measures. My father bought a book called *Pendlebury's Arithmetic* and I worked through its examples in long multiplication, long division and the rule of three. He marked my work and I did corrections. In addition to arithmetical rules I had to cope with Mr Pendlebury's pre-occupation with leaky baths and trains that foolishly ran towards each other from opposite ends of the same track. I also practised writing endlessly.

Usually when I arrived in a class after an absence or having been 'put up', I was placed at the bottom of the 'B' section. My aim was to get myself into the 'A' section as quickly as possible and be among those few who jockeyed week by week for the coveted place 'Top of the Class'. Before I left Bothal schools I had learned of some elusive, indefinable incitement, impossible to measure but of the utmost importance. To work and to qualify was not enough. In one particular class a girl held the top place week after week, and week after week when we'd shuffled round and everything was settled, she'd be given 2*d*. to go to a nearby sweet shop and buy a sugar pig as a reward for excellent work with conduct to match. More than being top, I wanted the dizzy euphoria of winning a sugar pig and taking it home to my mother. Life held for me no greater prize and I was only two places away. After a week of the utmost care and diligence, no talking, no nothing, I made it. I could hardly contain myself. I shook, literally, as the moment approached for me to go to the front, get the money and set off to buy the sugar pig. It never came. The moment was passed over as if it never had existed.

Similarly, in another class, I was placed in the 'B' section and a week later I had made the 'A' section at number eight. This, however, meant that one of those who had sat in this section hitherto had to move out. She was a very pretty girl with small features, large eyes and a mop of spun curls. She stood there, tears brimming her eyes. I thought the teacher was going to cry, too, she was so sorry for her. She looked at her 'A' section, and her gaze settled on me.

'You come out, Linda,' she said, 'and you can sit right at the back, at the very top of the "B" section.' Any tears that brimmed my eyes went unnoticed.

The following week I worked to the exclusion of all else: this time the issue could not be in doubt. I was top.

'From now on,' said the teacher, 'you will move up and down only in your sections. Those in section "A" will stay there. The same for section "B".'

It never occurred to me to complain at home, or even to think I had been unfairly treated. Obviously the fault lay somewhere in me. Rarely, indeed, did any child complain about having been punished at school. To do so almost certainly meant another punishment at home, in support of that already given at school, even if you were not absolutely sure what you had done wrong in the first place.

I recall one lesson when, for some reason, the teacher in Standard Six was missing. The curtain dividing Six and Five was drawn back. Those at the bottom end of Five were sent, somewhat glumly, to Standard Four to swell the ranks there. Those at the top end of the Six were sent, somewhat smugly, to Standard Seven. The remainder of Standard Six was squashed into Standard Five, so that the forms were filled to the point of suffocation. The remaining girls had to stand at the back and down the sides. In this crowded atmosphere without benefit of a kettle, water, heating appliance, cup or saucer, the teacher set about the lesson, the title of which she wrote on the blackboard – 'How to Make a Cup of Tea'.

Now, every girl present had imbibed the ability to make this beverage with her mother's milk, or with Glaxo, if the former was deficient. And tea was made to suit the man of the house. At the end of the meal, good tea was hardly ever thrown out but was left in the oven, or on the drop-down oven door for whoever looked upon stewed tea as a delicacy. In our house tea was made for a particular meal and the tea-pot cleaned out and put away with the tea things. I simply thought this was our idiosyncrasy. My grandmother Summers's tea-pot always had tea in it: that was hers.

As this instruction had to last over a whole period it is likely the teacher began with setting the table. She probably insisted on a clean white cloth and other unrealistic impedimenta. I do not know. I was concerned only in not making myself conspicuous and seeing that I got my quota of what air there was. Other than that, I gave myself up to wool-gathering. Suddenly, I was brought back to life. The teacher was cleaning the board, the lesson almost over.

'Now,' she said, pointing to a girl, 'how do you make a cup of tea?'

The girl stood up and looked at the ceiling that she might concentrate the better. Then she spoke.

'Forst. Empy the tea-pot.'

'You have not been listening, girl! Come out here.'

Accepting this vagary of life without malice, the girl went out, put out one hand, then the other and went back to her place, her tingling palms under her arm pits.

The teacher looked round the class.

'What did she say that was wrong?'

My hand shot up on the instant in common with the rest of the class, less one. I hadn't the least idea what she'd said wrong, but if I didn't put my hand up I would draw attention to myself, my state of ignorance would be brought to light and I, too, would be nursing tingling palms. This way the odds were in favour of my lack of knowledge passing unnoticed, especially if I extended my arm to its fullest length, waved my hand about, bobbed up and down and hissed, 'Miss, Miss,Miss,' as if I had the answer at my finger ends. If I'd actually been chosen, I'd have had to leave my answer to the inspiration of the moment.

Actually, this being the end of the lesson, the teacher would stretch out the coda for as long as necessary. If there was only a short time to go, she would choose those she knew had the right answers. She was no fool!

The year or so after I left school the system changed but, in my time, the 'scholarship class' consisted of those whom Miss Dixon considered would not only benefit from secondary school education, but whose parents would allow them to go to such a school should they qualify.

This was the one class Miss Dixon taught. We went in awe of her, but I don't remember her ever using the strap. What she believed in was backbone.

'Your trouble is,' she would say to some weeping recalcitrant standing before her, 'you have *no backbone*. Get yourself a bit of *backbone* and you'll be a lot better.'

'What I like about you,' she would beam approval on another, 'is you have *backbone*. And plenty of it. That's what I like to see.'

Scholarship classes were held on the side of Standard Six nearest the curtain. They lasted the whole of each morning of the term in which the scholarship was taken and consisted of mechanical arithmetic, mental arithmetic, problems, English exercises, composition and something called 'intelligence'. There were twelve in the class in my year, four of whom elected to go to Bedlington Secondary and one whose parents decided on Morpeth High. After the scholarship was over I, in company with one or two other girls, moved up into Standard Seven.

Backbone deficiency

3. The Rows

Where the miners smoked their pipes at the railings by the plantins, you could, instead of turning left, carry straight on. Eventually, this direction would bring you to the road crossing Booth's corner. On the left there was the colliery manager's house and, on the right, a huge black fence hiding from the eyes of the world the manager's garden. Beyond this, on the left, were the ends of the Rows, Second, Third, Fourth and Fifth and, on the right, the ends of the Ninth (the Eighth was behind the fence), Tenth and Eleventh Rows.

These Rows teemed with life and activity most of the time. Each house had a long garden and a yard. Some of the yards were covered in with a wooden structure called a 'back-end', always kept clean and bright by frequent painting and cleaning. The 'back-end' always had a stable door. Across the road from the houses were the middens – rectangular pits partially bricked up. The short walls of these pits each provided for two earth-closets, called netties.

No one talked of going to the loo, or the WC, or the lavatory, or toilet, the bog or the john. You went 'across the road' or, if you lived in the Second row, 'down the garden'. Where there was a large family, or a large gathering, it was quite a consideration going out on an icy winter's night or in heavy rain. When this happened someone might say, 'Is Kitty Bell at home?' and there would be a general count round to see if anyone was missing. If no one was missing then Kitty Bell was at home and the enquirer went 'across the road' knowing it would be vacant.

Into the midden, therefore, went all household refuse and human excreta. Next to these buildings were the coal-houses, and in some Rows, the wash-houses. Alongside the middens and wash-houses ran a two-foot rolley way where horses or ponies pulled iron bogies with moveable sides. These tubs delivered coals to the pit-men. They were tipped alongside the coal-house and either left for the man of the house on his return, shovelled in by the housewife herself, or the job given to a young out-of-work man who usually went round with his own shovel, asking, 'Can Aa shul yer coals in, Missus?' The place had to be swept and left clean after coals were in. The recognized payment for this was 3d., but some tried to get away with less, even offering as little as a slice of jam and bread (usually never accepted).

The same rolley way was used to clean out the middens and closets. Again, horses dragged bogies in which the effluent was placed. This unsavoury job was done at night by men officially called 'night-soil men' but, unofficially, 'midden men' or 'night riders'. When the middens were done away with, the bogies were changed for motorized waggons called 'foddens'.

The road between the middens and the houses was unmade – that is, it was a mass of clarty ruts and messy puddles and pools of water in spring, autumn and part of winter. In the very cold weather it was full of iron-hard, sharp ruts and in summer, a sea of dust. All this added to the housewife's difficulties in keeping her house clean.

At intervals along the Rows were well-built stand taps. These were often centres of friendly gossip and vantage-points from which to watch your neighbours' affairs, under guise of working. At least one romance started 'at the tap'. The taps also gave rise to the local joke, 'Where d'ye live?' 'Seven netties doon past the tap.'

It was usual to go to the tap for a rake of water – that is, two pails across which an iron square was placed to allow for a steady passage and less water spilling on the way back to the house.

Except on a Sunday, street vendors traversed the Rows. The rag-and-bone man with his flat cart and cry of 'Scrubby stones for owld stockin's,' fishmongers with their cry, 'Caller Harn. Caller Harn,' the scissor-grinder with his, 'Scissoers to grind. Bring oot yer gullies [carving knives].' Then there were butchers', bakers', and greengrocers' carts galore. The door-to-door pedlars still operated, but they were fast becoming obsolete.

Milk was delivered twice a day. In the morning, the horse-drawn float from the Colliery Farm or the Store Farm brought the large churns. Hanging from the rims of these churns were the measures which were used to fill the basin or jug brought out by the housewife. In hot weather, the milk was boiled almost straightaway to keep it from going sour. Most often, in the evening, a woman came round on foot with a yoke over her shoulders, suspended from which were two large cans. Fewer people bought milk at night.

Money to spend was something few children had, except on Saturdays. Instead of sweets, children were given a thick slice of 'jilly and breed' or some 'soor rut', the name sometimes given to rhubarb which grew in abundance in most gardens. They were given a stick of rhubarb and a piece of newspaper with a spoonful of sugar on it. The newspaper in one hand and the rhubarb in the other, they ran around, dipping the fruit into the sugar before they ate it.

In out-of-school hours children were to be seen everywhere playing 'round the doors', in summer in the roads, at the corner ends, in the lane at the back of the gardens, on top of the tap cover, on top of the coal-houses or in the wash-houses. In winter they usually played round the street lamp unless they were playing 'Jack Shine Yer Miggy'. Apart from back-lane cricket and football for the boys there were numerous other ball-games played by girls, among them 'Piney' and a game where you bounced the ball and went through a series of simple gymnastics as you did so. For girls also there were singing games – 'The Farmer's in his Den', 'Grandmother Grandmother Grey', 'Here's Poor Sally', 'The Big Ship Sails' among them.

In season, tops and whips were ubiquitous. The tops cost a halfpenny and the owners decorated them with coloured chalks so that they made a pretty pattern as they spun. Home-made whips were best. There were competitions to see who could whip a top furthest or keep it spinning longest. Skipping ropes were also popular and when the nights lengthened it was quite a common sight to see a long rope being turned across the road and women joining the girls in skipping. There was the communal 'All in by January, February . . . All out by January, February . . .' when you ran in to skip when your birthday month came up and ran out when it came round again. Some were very skilled and could do peppers and double peppers (skipping in a rope turned at great speed, or with two ropes being turned at speed in opposite directions). In the lane that separated one lot of gardens from another row of middens, girls sometimes played shops or houses with any broken bits of glass or crockery they had, but most often the lane belonged to the boys where they played Cowboys and Indians, marbles with penkers (the most prized of all marbles) or games with cigarette cards. Occasionally, they let out someone's pig or hens for the excitement of seeing the animal being caught and brought back. When this happened and the boys were caught the owner meted out punishment on the spot.

Two boys were once caught rifling through some boxes in the colliery yard. The 'collry pollis' caught them and asked their names and addresses. They were told to go back home and stay there till the policeman came and talked to them in the presence of their parents. There was a general feeling that if you were caught it was only fair that you should take your punishment.

Not all children were allowed out to play. This was particularly true of girls who had to help with the never-ending household chores. In most miners' houses, there were daily tasks: cleaning out the fire, emptying the ash pan, whitening the space into which it fitted under the fire, rubbing the grate, the brass, the fender and the irons (these last with powdered ashes), putting the mats out to be shaken and 'broomed' with a heavy-duty brush, scraping the mud off the pit boots and cleaning them (for however dirty they were at the end of the shift, all miners started the new shift with shining footwear), dadding the pit clothes – that is, banging each article against the wall to remove as much of the coal dust as possible – getting in water, filling the set pot and the kit for the miner home from the pit, emptying it, and, of course, providing for meals, sometimes for miners at odd times of the day, cleaning the men's shoes till they shone and putting away their weekday suits in case they got 'cramped' (creased).

Monday was washday. The decks were cleared for action, the candle lit in the wash-house by five in the morning because there was friendly rivalry about who should get a line of washing out first. The set pot had to be filled and small fire under it lit. This was usually done by bringing two or three shovels full of live coals from the kitchen fire. Other items for this exercise were a bench on which to scrub clothes, a hefty scrubbing brush, a poss barrel, poss-stick, large mangle and a quantity of blue-mottled or white Windsor soap. Hard soap was scraped into the set-pot and the poss barrel, the latter one-third full of hot water. The poss-stick was a wooden contraption about three-feet high with a small T-bar to act as handles and a heavy bottom with four slits. To poss, you grasped the handle firmly and lifted the stick up and down, thumping the clothes. Where there were two women there were usually two poss-sticks so that they could double-poss, i.e. work in rhythm, one coming down as the other went up. Whites had to be possed, scrubbed, boiled, dipped in dolly blue, mangled and, sometimes, starched after they'd been dried. Last of all, the pit clothes were washed. When everything was finished and all the clothes blowing on the line in the garden or draped round clothes horses in the house, the set pot had to be emptied with a ladle and cleaned out, the fire raked out and cleaned, the poss barrel emptied and dried out, the mangle rubbed down, the stone floor scrubbed and patterned round the edges with donkey stone or scrubby stone and the step scrubbed and similarly adorned or 'red rudded' and then rubbed over with sour milk. A worn mat was thoroughly shaken and broomed and put into place on the floor. After they were dried, the clothes were often mangled again before they were ironed. This ironing was done on the kitchen table over a blanket and part of an old sheet. Most people used a box iron, either large or small. The internal bit was heated in the fire till it was red hot, lifted skilfully out with the poker and placed in the box part of the iron and shut in. Two of these insides used alternately were the bare minimum.

The washing took preference over everything else on a Monday and family life suffered under its tyranny. Food was anything which could be hurriedly prepared. Wet washing days were an absolute misery. The house was full of damp, steaming clothes and no comfort anywhere. Yet, incredibly, some fun could be wrung out of this exercise as when young girls espied favoured young lads coming home from the pit. The girl took a handful of suds from the end of the poss-stick and threw it at the lad who pretended to be annoyed, smiling, 'Aa'll get ye fer that.' Even so, the victim went on walking taller and more briskly because he had been singled out. The main meal on Monday was cold meat and fried potatoes and vegetables left over from Sunday with any left-over rice pudding and any left-over cakes.

Tuesday was baking day. Years earlier, families went direct to the station when flour came in and carried their own sacks away to be paid for later. Each house had a flour bin, a bread bin and a huge earthenware bread dish, for bread was hardly ever bought. The smell on a baking day was heavenly. Large freshly baked loaves cooling the length of the settle and on the window sill, fadges [flat rounds of bread] teacakes, scones and a delicious flat cake full of currants called 'Pushy-up Cake'. This last was eaten straight from the oven and it swam in melted butter. Perhaps this was the root cause of what Aunt Jean used to call, 'The Summers' Stomach'. The way she said it it sounded like a rare national achievement awarded only to members of our family. The main meal on Tuesdays was Pan Haggerty (or Hagglety) made of thin slices of potatoes, onions and cold meat cooked in water in a large frying pan. The was followed by newly baked teacakes and any Pushy-up Cake still remaining. Years later, I asked Auntie Anna how this delicacy was made. 'I have no idea,' she said. 'That's why me mother called it Pushy-up Cake. She just pushed it up in a minute with anything that was handy.'

Wednesday was the day the bedrooms were done and the broth was made. Bones were boiled in an enormous iron pan that obliterated both fire and hob. After they were taken out, every type of vegetable imaginable, plus a plentiful supply of soaked dried peas, was added. This broth formed a goodly part of the staple diet till Saturday With each succeeding day it was reheated till it was just a solid mass of vegetables.

Thursday was the day of cleaning the front room plus some supplementary baking. Friday it was the kitchen and the pantry and all the brasses, the black-leading, the nettie and the yard. The wooden box, seat and lid was scrubbed in the nettie, the floor scrubbed and adorned with donkey stone and a fresh supply of cut newspaper suspended from the nail by a bit of yellow string, an additional supply of uncut sheets being placed on the flat bit of the closet for emergencies.

Saturday morning was the time for baking meat pies, fruit tarts and cakes. There was always a tea–dinner on Saturday and the afternoon for women was given over to a leisurely look at the shops, or a leisurely toilet in preparation for a look at the shops after tea, or any other amusement on offer. The only amusement some busy housewives got was to change into a clean pinny on Saturday night and lean on the yard gate or the back-end stable door and chat to anyone in the vicinity.

From spring till the beginning of winter every house had at least one fly paper, those captives adhering to the surface being but a fraction of those still alive whose Mecca was the pantry. Remembering the middens and earth closets, their diet was indeed, varied. The middens were replaced by bins and the earth closets by flush toilets very early in my life and I was a very tiny part of the cause of this change. There was an outbreak of small-pox to which I fell victim. I only remember getting up one morning and feeling dreadfully ill. Then I had a dream which was so vivid I remember every detail even yet. I was standing at the open back door of our house. Crowded behind me were all the members of our extended family. I looked up to a dark sky and a white boat, light as thistledown, floated towards me, a slim woman in white flowing robes at the helm. She put out her hands to me and joyfully I raised mine and floated up light as air, leaving my heavy body behind. My mother and father cried out, reached up and pulled me back, dragging me down. I struggled to be free and once again floated up towards the woman holding out her hands. Again the crying and again the pulling back, not only by my parents, but by others who were there. I struggled with them all, begging them to let me go. When I looked up, the woman and the boat had gone and I cried bitterly.

I opened my eyes with difficulty. Everything was so far away. The bed was huge and miles away, at the end of it, was my mother crying and with her my father. A woman was leaning towards me.

'You're a very important little girl,' she said. 'Three doctors have been here to see you and you knew nothing at all about it. Nothing they did could wake you up.'

When next I opened my eyes the first thing I was aware of was a strong smell of chloride of lime. I was in a strange bed and a woman (a nurse) was sitting beside me.

She stroked my forehead.

'Do you want anything?' she asked.

'The Salvation Army,' I said and closed my eyes.

How long it was before I was picked up, wrapped up and taken to the window, I don't know.

'Look,' said the nurse, pointing. I looked and there beyond the railings, was the Salvation Army. I leaned my head against that of the nurse. All I longed for was to go back to bed.

'They're waving to you,' she said, and so they were. 'Wave back,' she went on. I did so. 'Does that make you feel better?' she asked as they played. I nodded.

What had happened was that I'd been taken by horse-drawn ambulance to Pity Me, the isolation hospital near North Seaton. All my clothes and toys were burned. A white poster with a red cross was pasted on the wall at the side of both the front and back doors of the house which was fumigated. My parents and my brother were vaccinated. All three were quite ill for several days.

When I began to take more of an interest in what was happening I realized I had a fair covering of spots about my person. Originally, these were yellow and soft. They were dabbed with 'dope' two or three times a day and gradually they became brown and hard. By this time I was out of bed and walking around. I realized I wasn't the only one in the hospital; there were quite a number of all ages and both sexes. It was constantly drummed into us that we must not touch our spots but must let them drop off spontaneously when they would leave no scars. We could not leave hospital till all our spots had gone.

I had one to go, just below my right ankle. Unfortunately, it was knocked off by accident, a fact which was not realized till many hours afterwards when the area had become infected. It was back to bed and, as the days passed, the number of patients dwindled, till finally, the doctor looked at the scab on my foot and pronounced me fit.

I had had a steady flow of sweets, toys, books, eggs and fruit while I'd been in hospital and my father telephoned every day. Everything belonging to me had to be left behind. A nurse bathed me. Another examination and I was wrapped in a towel and taken to another room. There was my mother, smiling. She handed my brand-new clothes to the nurse who dressed me and hand in hand with my mother, I set out for home. My joy was short-lived. My ankle was still infected, my foot now red and swollen. Angry red marks were creeping up my leg, my head ached and I was on fire.

'I'm afraid,' said Dr McLean, 'it's back to the hospital.'

I cried, my mother cried and Dr McLean said he would see what he could do at home. I had blood poisoning. Thereafter for months, it was abscess after abscess on my legs and on my head and my arms. And there seemed no end to the throbbing pain, the headaches, the sickness, the red-hot rising temperature and the shivering, chilling drop, the hot bathings, the hot fomentations, the trips to the out-patients' department of Ashington Hospital, the waiting when I cried without ceasing, my mother upset and helpless and near to fainting, the screaming as I was taken away to have my head partially shaved and the offending abscess lanced; my father's taking me from then on because it upset my mother too much, his caring, helpless unease, the awful medicine, the dressings, the smell, the firm hands and stiff white bosoms of the nurses, the moment when the dressings were quickly pulled off, those awful red marks for ever climbing my leg or my arm.

There is always some kindly soul who offers a known cure when nothing else seems to be working. This 'cure' was Dale's Plaster, a hard black substance rather like sealing wax in texture and in that it had to be melted. It was held over the offending eruption this time sited at the top of my right leg. A match was struck and the hot molten fluid dropped dead centre. They didn't land another. I yelled fit to waken the dead and kicked myself free. It possibly cured the abscess: I no longer have it, though I do have the scar. After an absence of about a year I went back to school. But there were further outbreaks. I seemed to have a permanent sick headache (except when I was at Wooler) and the almost daily consideration was whether or not it was bad enough to keep me off school.

Gradually, the period between each attack lengthened and when I was nine I put in my first term of unbroken attendance, not without a struggle. At the time, both my hands were bandaged and my vigilance for tell-tale red marks unceasing. But I had reached Standard Five and I had my sights on the scholarship class. I was afraid my poor attendance record might militate against this, so when Miss Dixon came into the classroom I thought I would bring my triumph to her notice, and put up my hand.

'Yes?' she said.

'Please, Miss Dixon,' I said, 'I've put in a full attendance this term. I've never been absent and never late.'

'I can see nothing unusual in that, Linda,' she replied. 'Many girls are neither late nor absent during their whole school lives.'

Even in small matters swollen heads had to be reduced in size lest worse befell.

Gradually, the blood poisoning disappeared altogether and several years were to pass before, just after the Second World War, I had another attack. I had grazed my hand. It became red and angry-looking and the thin red line began its climb up my arm. I rang the doctor.

'Don't do a thing,' he said, 'till I come round.' He looked at my arm. 'Yes,' he said. 'You were right. But watch this.' He prepared a syringe, dabbed my arm with antiseptic, plunged in the needle, took it out and threw it away together with the empty phial, packed his bag, washed his hands and sat down to chat.

'How do you feel?' he asked after a time.

'My arm's a bit stiff, but I feel a lot better.'

He looked at my arm. The red mark was in retreat. 'That's it,' he said. 'That's penicillin. Isn't it marvellous?' I could only agree.

The next morning the mark was back again.

'The dose wasn't strong enough,' the doctor said when I told him. 'We'll try again.' The second jab worked like a charm.

The day for the coals

4. 29 the Ninth

My grandparents lived at 29 Ninth Row. This was a double row occupied by families where there were two or more workers at the pit. Number 29 had been a chemist's in the early days when all shops were in the Rows; the large picture window with its ornate sides and heavy front door still remained, as did the short wall, paved area and side gate marking off the shop area. One day, almost 30 years after it had ceased to operate as a shop, a man knocked at the front door, handed in a large blue bottle and asked if he could have some more of that stomach bottle for it had done him a power of good!

At the back there was a yard and from one of its walls a zinc bath (the kit) was suspended from a nail. In the corner of the yard was the sink. Like every other house in the Rows, the small walk-in pantry had a tiny window facing the road. On the ledge of this window, the housewife placed her collection of egg-cups, most of which were elaborately fashioned. As we children walked down the Rows, we looked at these displays as we would at shop windows. Some stone window ledges were painted cream.

The back door of my grandmother's house opened straight on to a passage way about one-yard square. Even this area was partially used up by the everyday coats and caps that hung on the nail behind the door. A lot of women called the coat they kept here 'me coat for gannin t' the store'.

Like most houses in the Rows, my grandmother's door was hardly ever locked, and, on the rare occasions when it was, you simply lifted the bottom part of the window up a little and felt along till you got the key. No one ever thought of using the front door except to go down the garden.

Straight ahead of you, as you opened the back door at Number 29 was a steep flight of narrow stairs on the left-hand side of which, one pair to a stair, were the shining clean weekday boots and shoes of the family.

The door to the immediate right led to the kitchen and the first thing that caught your eye when you opened that door was the huge kitchen range which occupied slightly more than half of the opposite wall. It was a symphony of shining black, matt white, silver grey and burnished brass. The central part was the hot fire which, following superstition, was never allowed to go out. Rarely did one put a shovel of coals on the fire unless it was a shovel of duff to allow the fire to burn slowly overnight. Almost always a pail of coal (sometimes two) was 'hoyed' (thrown) to the back of the fire and raked down as necessary with the 'colrake' (coal rake) a useful article usually made at the colliery. The other appurtenance to a good fire was the 'bleezer' (blazer), a flat sheet of metal slightly larger than the opening of the fire with a handle somewhere in the centre. The 'bleezer' was rested on the hob so that a draught was created and the fire burned more quickly and fiercely. Some people dispensed with the 'bleezer' and put a sheet of newspaper over the opening, snatching it away the second before it would have burst into flames. A black kettle sang almost permanently on the hob. On the right of the fire was the small set pot for hot water and, on the left, the circular oven with its drop-down door.

Above the fire was a brass rail often with a kettle-holder dangling from one end, and sometimes, if there were children in the house, a belt. Most often, though, the brass rail was used to dry off wet tea-towels or to keep underwear warm for the person who was bathing in front of the fire. Over the brass rail was the mantelpiece, where the tea caddy stood together with, possibly, an alarm clock, a pen and a bottle of ink and – invariably – several ornaments and a pair of brass candlesticks. Some people had plush bobble-fringes suspended from the mantelpiece. On the hearth was the fender and fire irons. Many people had an ornate Sunday fender and fire irons in addition to the steel weekday ones. As my grandmother had a sitting-room, she had only one kitchen fender.

The best mat in my grandmother's kitchen was immediately in front of the fire. On the wall adjacent to the fireplace there was a settle, a long wooden bench set against the wall with a partition at the end to ward off draughts. Opposite the fireplace was the chest of drawers with its big chiming clock and the family Bible. On weekdays when my grandfather returned from anywhere other than work, he hung his cap on the nail behind the door and started undoing his collar-stud. By the time he had reached the chest of drawers he had released himself from the combined restrictions of his dicky, stiff white collar and dark tie. These articles he placed on the chest of drawers behind the clock. On Sundays he wore his black Dobson (Dop) hat. This was laid on top of the sewing machine when he came in. Like my father, he never wore gloves however cold the weather: it was effeminate to do so. In fact, also like my father, he wore practically the same weight of clothes summer and winter alike.

Next to the chest of drawers was the 'glory hole', which was really the under-the-stairs area. In this dark cubby-hole all the pit clothes and the house cleaning materials were kept. The sewing machine was on the wall adjacent to the glory hole. The only other items of furniture were the long kitchen table covered in dark American cloth, the form that ran alongside it below the window, three chairs, a carver, my grandfather's large Windsor chair, my grandmother's smaller spring rocking chair and the cracket (stool). Next to the fireplace was the closet on the top shelf in which I had an early glimpse of two leeches. After that they disappeared. They were in a glass jar together with other things on the top shelf of the cupboard. They were kept there to be put on a wound or a bruise to suck out the 'bad blood'. Next to that was the walk-in pantry. All water had to be carried. In the extreme corner on the right was a chair minus its back. On this chair was a tin dish with approximately three inches of cold water and a saucer containing a piece of blue mottled soap and a thick slippery piece of grey flannel. Two towels – one ordinary, one 'bratty' (a sort of sacking) – hung behind the pantry door. This tin dish was used for all hand-washing and face-wiping: the water in it was changed every morning. By the afternoon the water was decidedly grey and gritty and as the week wore on the towel began to vie with the flannel in slipperiness. The bratty towel was coarse and was used for the pit baths. The floor here and in the kitchen was made of stone; in the kitchen it was covered with linoleum and overlaid with mats. The linoleum tended to get worn so that by the time it was ready to be replaced it was in bits and difficult to scrub. There was, then, almost as much stone to scrub as lino. As she had a front room, my grandmother's kitchen mats were already on the downward grade, the one nearest the door being almost ready for its final demotion to the wash-house.

The front room had a black decorative fireplace with a tile surround and an ornate fender with brass knobs and huge brass fire irons. Over the fireplace was a mantelshelf with a plush bobble-fringe and above that a huge overmantel with a central looking-glass and little shelves going from the sides up to the top containing a myriad china ornaments.

One side of the room was completely taken up with a brass tester bed with its high bedhead, billowing white draperies and valance and its ornate quilt. Next to it were the tall-boys on top of which were huge ornaments that looked as if they were made of grey pebble-dash with splodges of red and green. Apart form those ornaments, anything that had to be kept out of reach was put on top of the tall-boys.

The huge 'shop window' area had an aspidistra on a stand and immediately before it a large black horse-hair sofa of ultra unyielding, ultra uncomfortable properties. In the corner of the room was an upright piano and behind this instrument, as though it were in disgrace, a zither. I think it was kept out of sight because no one wanted to be continually brought face to face with native ignorance regarding this musical enigma. No one knew what it was, how it should be played or who had bought it in the first place.

In the centre of the room was a round table with a plush cloth and four horse-hair dining chairs. Two armchairs stood before the fire and the wall space remaining was taken up with a Victorian sideboard and its burden of ornaments and photographs in frames. A large carpet square covered the floor, but this was so protected by mats that it was almost completely hidden from view.

Apart from a plaster-moulded picture of Robbie Burns's cottage which hung in the kitchen, all pictures in both rooms had been painted by my father's uncle, Geordie. Uncle Geordie was a curious mixture of real talent and self-effacing reticence unfitted for the cut and thrust of competitive, and sometimes aggressive, day-to-day living. Never having had an art lesson or a music lesson and almost blind for the greater part of his life, he nevertheless painted in oils and not only did he play the organ, the concertina and the melodeon, but he wrote music and made rolls of music on bits of paper for mechanical pianos and organs.

When my grandmother had a mat in the frames were propped up on the wall next to the sewing machine. Proggy (or clippy)

A mat in

mats were made with short clippings approximately two-and-a-half inches long, while hookey mats were made from long narrow lengths of looped cloth. As the materials for the mats were very often old clothes either given 'for a mat' or so outworn that they could no longer be 'made-over', the possible designs were limited and many mat-makers had to be content with a black border outlined in red and a 'mixy middle'. My Great Aunt Martha raised mat-making and quilt-making to an art. She bought materials and wrought beautiful designs with her handiwork. When the latest mat was unrolled for my mother's inspection and brother Billy and I stood waiting for our 'roll', we knew it would be a brief and careful affair – unlike the rolls we were allowed at my grandmother's who often left the new mat lying on the floor for about 15 minutes for us to roll to our hearts' content. These mats were thick and warm and heavy and sufficiently soft for 'rolling' to be a child's delight.

I could never understand why Sunday was the first day of the week. In the Catechism, which we repeated regularly, it said 'six days shalt thou labour – and rest the seventh day.' We rested the first day when work was kept to a minimum.

My grandmother got up in time to go to early communion and returned to clean the fire, do the mats and make breakfast as and when it was needed for other members of the family. She was helped in all this work by her daughter, my Auntie Anna, until the latter got married. My grandfather went to the club or the Portland and returned for his meal at about one o'clock. He sat at the head of the table in the carver chair which he filled to capacity. He was flanked on either side by his sons, places being left for my aunt and grandmother. First he had a large crisp Yorkshire Pudding which he ate with sugar and milk, using a knife and fork. The others had a smaller portion of Yorkshire Pudding with gravy. Then followed the main course, usually roast beef. My grandfather's large dinner plate would be piled high with meat, turnips, peas, cabbage or Brussels sprouts, roast potatoes, mashed potatoes and gravy. My uncles would be served after him and, lastly, the women folk of the family. My grandmother carved. There was always rice pudding to follow after which the men went to their favourite spot (if they weren't going out) where they read the Sunday papers and had a cup of tea brought to them. By the time their cup was taken away to be washed, they were asleep. When all the dishes were washed my grandmother was at liberty to go and lie down and my aunt to prepare her toilet, so that she was dressed in her best at tea-time.

When she was ready Auntie Anna came downstairs and set the table for tea. Bread, butter, jam, Edam cheese, teacake, scones, wholemeal loaf, rice loaf, rhubarb or apple tart, custard tart, spice (fruit) loaf, cream cakes, pears and evaporated milk. By the time she was finished everyone was awake making wry mouths and ready for tea. As a family we often went to tea on Sundays. We children had to eat one piece of bread and butter and one piece of bread, butter and jam before we were allowed to have any cheese. When we were given a piece, my grandmother would say, 'Remember, a little bit of cheese and a big bite of bread.' Rarely were we offered a free choice. Instead, it was, 'Would you like a piece of teacake or a scone?' or 'Would you care for rhubarb tart or custard tart?'

The cream cakes, for us, were out. My favourite fare after that was the custard tart, delicious creamy egg custard an inch-and-a-half thick and wonderful shortcrust pastry. I could hardly enjoy what went before in case I wasn't going to be offered a piece of custard tart. We did get a small helping of pears and 'cream'. If the table was full of adults, which it usually was, my brother and I had our meal sitting on cushions on the floor and eating off the settle. I didn't mind at all (I rather enjoy working my way up from the bottom in the hierarchy of things), but I don't think my brother liked this indignity one little bit.

My grandfather would go systematically round the table sampling everything it had to offer, then he'd say, 'Ye know, I'm no hand for this sort of stuff. Haddaway into the pantry, Lizzie, and cut me a meat sandwich' (i.e. two meat sandwiches).

On Sunday evenings the house was usually full as those who were courting brought their 'intendeds'. Auntie Anna was an accomplished pianist and we sang (or rather, the adults sang) to her accompaniment. Often the men would whistle or beat out a drum rhythm on the table with an upturned plate and two knives.

There were special Sundays, one of which was 'Carlin Sunday'. It took place during Lent, and in fact coincided with Mothering Sunday which we did not then celebrate. Carlins were brown peas soaked overnight, boiled and then fried in butter and sugar. They were eaten in the evening and every club and public house in the area had a plentiful supply for customers. They were delicious but they gave rise to the rhyme: *'Carlin Sunday/Poop-poop Monday.'* I was told that the custom derived from a time of great famine when no food had been eaten in the area for weeks. A boat was shipwrecked off the coast and its cargo of carlins washed ashore, thus providing the locals with their first food for ages. The story is probably apocryphal. For the rest of the year they were called grey peas and were fed uncooked to pigeons.

5. The Pit and the Store

The pit was one of the dominant factors in our lives. It began as soon as you passed the row of outhouses belonging to the Eleventh Row. Here were to be seen the colliery garages which gave way to the pit yard. Like the church, this had been part of my life from the beginning. I can remember making my first acquaintance with school, but I cannot remember my first excursion over the coal-dusted railway lines and up the iron staircase to the telephone exchange where my father worked, to give him his bait. This leads me to suppose that I first went there in my mother's arms. My father only had bait taken to him on certain shifts, most likely double shifts, or when he had a bilious attack. I think this was because, on these occasions, the meal was a hot one and so was the tea. At least they were when the messenger set out. But, especially on a winter's night, when they were most needed, every vestige of warmth must have evaporated by the time the destination was reached.

The pit was dark, solid and for ever. It supplied the money on which the community lived. Yet, it was a fickle master. My

Colliery telephone exchange

father, being a safety man, worked regularly, but, for many of the others, a full week's work was by no means a certainty. The end of each day marked 'buzzer time'. Each pit had its own time, but if the buzzer blew four times at eight o'clock, it meant that all

Bait tin   Bait bottle

pits in the area were idle next day. Thereafter, Penker's Drift
blew at 8.45pm, all Woodhorn 9.0pm, Bothal 6.0pm, Duke
7.30pm and Carl 7.0pm.

Returning and passing along the other side of the black-tarred
fence would allow you to see the end of the Eighth Row and the
end of the Seventh Row and after it, the store. The first thing
you would actually see belonging to the store would be the open
doors of the cobbled grocery yard. Here was a proliferation of
empty boxes, many of them made of wood, bits of paper and
rough, yellow string. Here, also, a horse usually stood between
the shafts of a cart, patiently waiting to be loaded up.

Among my contemporaries, the brave and reckless who went
into the yard were sometimes rewarded with an empty box or,
more often, a wooden gourd (i.e. a wooden hoop from a Danish
butter cask). My own particular treasure among empty boxes
was a Woodbine box, the kind that, when full, held twopenny
packets of Woodbines.

From the grocery yard doors a solid brick wall led you to the
corner where the premises of the Ashington Industrial Co-
operative Society were to be seen in all their solid worth. First,
the stairs leading to the drapery department, the entrance to
which was marked by two doors, whose glass upper portions
were emblazoned with inflowing script: 'Gowns and Mantles'.
Below and next to the drapery opening was the huge grocery
department, then the butchery and, adjacent to it, the hardware
followed by the greengrocery departments. Between the hardware and the greengrocery there was a narrow alleyway, on the
left of which was an opening which led to the door and a flight of

stairs. At the top of the stairs, on the left, was the bespoke tailoring department and, on the right, a warren of rooms where meetings of all kinds were held for young and old.

Also, somewhere in this alleyway, there was a cobbler's shop, but my memory of this is hazy because I never went there. My father cobbled our shoes at home. He was neither particularly happy at this job, nor particularly skilled in it, but it was his duty as paterfamilias.

The bakery department had been moved to premises on the opposite side of the road, nearer the Portland Hotel. This was another department I knew little about because my mother made all our bread, cakes, pastries and pies. We never had 'bought stuff' on the table. My grandmother, on the other hand, paid regular trips to the bakery on Saturdays to buy her box of cream cakes for Sunday tea.

True, the real headquarters was at Hirst and a striking building it was. No other store in the area had such imposing headquarters. The pillared entrance was flanked by each department's shops so that there was a pleasant covered-in spacious arcade. At the top of the arcade there was a wide sweep of marble stairs which divided into two flights, one to the left and one to the right, each flight framed in an ornate marble balustrade. The stairs led to a wide balcony which ran alongside the general office and the boardroom. On one side of these rooms was the millinery and dress department and, on the other, the check office. On the next floor up was the ball-room, its ancillary rooms and the café.

My family, the church, the school, the pit and the store. These were woven into the fabric of my life from the beginning. Allegiance to the church might waver, schools change, our stay in various houses be short-lived, work at the pit be unpredictable but our attitude to the store was steadfast. It claimed our whole-hearted fealty and esteem. The Ashington Industrial Co-operative Society was the largest store in Northumberland because it played such a large part in our considerable community.

6. Shifting

As I said, I did not live long in Station Road. The coal company wished to give its employees the opportunity to buy their own houses and the estate on which they were built became known as the Colliery Scheme. At that time the government allowed builders £100 for each house they built. The colliery decided to make this payment immediately to each employee who bought a house. Thus the price of the most expensive houses, £485, became £385. The interest was 3 per cent and the deposit required was £5. My parents opted to buy 16 Ashbourne Crescent. We didn't move house, we shifted. Like everyone else we accomplished this on a Saturday afternoon when most men would be off work. My parents did not ask for help, but our relatives came as a matter of course. My mother and some of the women went to the new house. My father was nominally in charge of the old. My grandmother and my Aunt Bella stayed with him to tidy up after the furniture had gone, although my mother had already scrubbed the place within an inch of its life against the arrival of the incoming tenants. Billy and I had been told to behave and keep out of the way and knowing the consequences of disobedience, we obeyed. We waited for the man who was going to shift the furniture. At two o'clock he arrived, bringing with him a flat cart pulled by a small frail horse, scant of flesh and full of years. When he wasn't shifting furniture the man was a rag-and-bone merchant and among the empty sacks on the cart was a small pile of worn and grubby garments and an old bed rail which he had collected on his way to our house. He was also an opportunist.

The business having fairly commenced, we got out of the way and stood on the pavement where we were shortly joined by a small group of children who kept a respectful distance. Fortunately, it was a fine day and male passers-by remarked on this fact to my father.

'You've getten a fine day there, Arch,' they said in a congratulatory tone as though my father had personally and with wisdom selected this weather when a careless or thoughtless man might have chosen rain, sleet, snow or a high wind. Some men stopped to offer advice as a piece of furniture was being manoeuvred through the front door. The awkward furniture was always considered to be feminine.

You've brought her out the wrong way

'Bring her ower to the right a bit . . . no that's ower far . . . to the left, *left* . . . canny, now, canny . . . no, you'll have to take her back in and turn her round.'

To my private pride, the first item out was the wardrobe. Until this moment it had been housed in my parent's room, but as they were to have a brand-new bedroom suite, already installed in the new house, I was to have their old one – or rather, part of it. Half of it, my mother decided should go to me and half to my brother – he pointed out that he wasn't getting half, he was only getting the drawers, while I was getting the wardrobe and the wash stand. My mother said that when you halved three you got a big half and a little half and added that I had to get the big half because I was a girl. Apparently, there were some advantages to being a girl. I was glad of it. It was the only one I'd noticed so far.

It was a cumbersome piece of furniture and took some getting through the door. Out in the open it did not seem quite as imposing as it had in the house and when it finally lay on its back, draped here and there with protective bits of sacking, it looked only slightly superior to the discarded bed rail.

At this point Uncle Kit gave Billy a penny to be shared with me. We ran to the nearest shop, although we knew for certain that you got less for your money there than at the one further along.

'I want gob-stoppers,' Billy said as we ran.

'Pontefract cakes,' I panted. Normally, it would have taken us two hours to reach this decision, although at that time I had a passion for Pontefract cakes and rarely bought anything else.

Miss Davidson's shop was sparsely stocked and trade was far from brisk, yet she took her time in coming from the back shop. She served with the air of a reluctant Lady of the Manor doing her duty by the serfs. She carried no orange stuck with cloves before her, but you wouldn't have been surprised to see one.

'If you please, Miss Davidson,' we asked, 'may we have two gob-stoppers and a ha'penny-worth of Pomfret cakes?' If you didn't ask politely she made you ask again.

She considered the request and said, 'It would be better if you spoke one at a time.' It was no good trying to hurry, it only made things worse.

'Two gob-stoppers please, Miss Davidson,' Billy requested. She went slowly to the window. 'A red one and a blue one,' he added, tacking on hastily as she turned to come back, 'please.'

She weighed my Pontefract cakes slowly and with great care, replacing a larger one with a small when the needle stopped moving. I watched her every movement. Back at the house the cart was rapidly becoming laden. Billy examined his gob-stoppers and selected the blue one. From time to time he removed it from his mouth to inspect the changing colour. I halved my sweets to make them go further and gingerly ate one piece.

'I always buy gob-stoppers,' remarked one of the boy onlookers. 'They last a long time.'

'Me, too,' the boy next to him agreed. We heard, but took no notice. To have even acknowledged their presence would have meant they would have immediately attached themselves to us as friends and we knew what *that* meant.

At last the first load was ready. Uncle Kit, Uncle Jack and Uncle Will dusted themselves down and set off for the new house to be ready to greet the cart when it arrived. The furniture was tied down with some lengths of very knotted rope, the rag-and-bone man said, 'Gee-up there,' to his horse which summoned every rheumatic sinew and finally got the cartwheels revolving. We followed behind at a respectful distance and, even then, I could not help observing that the cartload of furniture denuded of its familiar background looked little different from his normal merchandise. We arrived at the new house. My uncles, who had got there before us, came out and unloaded the furniture on to the pavement and the concrete path leading to the back door. Last of all came the wardrobe.

'She'll not go in the back. We'll have to take her round the front,' said Uncle Kit and they manoeuvred it round the side of the house. At the front door they paused for breath and surveyed the entrance passage and the stairs they had to negotiate. Uncle Kit shook his head. At that my mother came out briskly.

'It all comes to pieces. Here, here and here,' she said, giving it a few expert taps and departed as briskly as she'd come.

The rag-and-bone man prepared to return for the second load. We stood expectantly. It was the moment we had waited for and anticipated since we had first learned we were going to shift. He made himself a seat with the sacks and then looked at us.

'Do you want a ride?' he asked. Billy was up almost before he'd finished saying, 'Yes, please.' I was lifted up and put in the middle of the cart. We looked around, pleased with ourselves, but grinning rather self-consciously. The man slapped the horse with the reins, said, 'Gee-up, there,' and we were off. Relieved of his load, the horse went at a brisk trot. My brother, who was referred to as 'a real bonnie lad' to denote his robust appearance and health, sat on the edge of the cart with his feet dangling, enjoying every second. My weight, on the other hand, was negligible and my smile was more than a little fixed as I bounced up and down as though I were a cork. The horse which had seemed so small and frail now seemed enormous and full of life as I stretched forward to clutch the edge of the cart. Then it lifted its tail and did something which I thought was excessively rude. When it had finished the man said, 'Whoa, there'; taking a pail which was hanging below the cart, he went back and scooped up what he justly considered was his. I used the brief respite to grasp a finer hold of the edge. When we arrived back at the old house the second load was already awaiting us on the pavement so the turn-around was quite quick.

I had no desire for a further trip on the cart nor was I particularly interested in the third load, the mangle and its bed-fellows.

I did not hear you say 'Please'

7. *The Store Order Man*

It is fitting that my first encounter with someone working in the store opposite should be the store order man, for it was the store order man who first brought Co-operation to Ashington. This missionary came from the West Sleekburn branch of Cramlington Co-operative Society. Crossing the river, he took orders for all the necessities of life required at Fell-em-Doon and he continued to travel there in spite of itinerant hawkers and small traders.

In 1875, in true Rochdale tradition (although this latter probably had much more than £14), Cramlington Store opened a branch shop in Fell-em-Doon in a house in Cross Row, number 1½. Perhaps these pioneers lingered too long in

Store order man bringing Co-operation

establishing themselves because competition was soon made manifest by the opening of the New Pit Store in 1876. This new shop apparently paid better dividends than the one in Cross Row and the latter shop ceased trading after a while. Ashington New Pit Store had its premises in High Market and the pit referred to was probably Bothal Pit. There were 490 members, John Craig was the general manager, and the Society catered for groceries, provisions, butcher meat, draperies, millinery, dress- and mantle-making and boot- and shoe-making.

Shortly after this, another store opened its doors. This was the Old Pit Store and here the pit referred to was probably Fell-em-Doon. The new enterprise was built in Ellington Terrace in the grounds of a bungalow. The grounds were called 'The Garden of Wood' because the man living in the bungalow was called Wood. It was situated next to the granary where choppy (chopped hay with crushed oats) was made for the pit. James Drysdale was the general manager and its secretary was Edward Gregory, Master Shifter, of 36 Fourth Row. The latter was also organist at the Primitive Methodists and secretary to the trustees of the Methodist Chapel. In 1876 there were two Methodist Chapels.

The Old Pit Store sold groceries, millinery, dress materials, provisions and boots and shoes.

As yet, both of these Societies were in Bothal Desmene because, until the building of the Church of the Holy Sepulchre, Ashington had no separate identity. By 1881, the population of Ashington had risen to 2,091.

The New Pit Store branched out first and established a branch at Pegswood. Later, Pegswood had its own society. As an aside, I am told that the members of the committee of this store were given a 'nice apple' each as payment for their services.

In the meantime, the New Pit Store built new premises. These buildings became the headquarters of the Ashington Industrial Co-operative Society when the two Pit Stores, Old and New, amalgamated in 1881. These were the premises I saw as I looked out of the bedroom window when I was a small child.

In the early days, trading must have been carried on in what became the grocery department. There was a lecture hall capable of seating 800. There was also a Temperance Hotel, the manager of which was William Crawford. This last building was overshadowed by the nearby Portland Hotel, built in 1885. However, the Co-op Temperance Hotel was still operating in 1887, after which it seems to have faded from the scene. The hardware, greengrocery and tailoring departments were added, together with another hall. This tailoring department was not to be confused with the 'bespoke tailoring', which was a different thing altogether. Apparently, the bespoke tailoring was an adjunct of the drapery department. This was because the 'men's tailoring' refused to have anything to do with the bespoke trade.

After the building of the second hall, the drapery department moved into the old hall.

In 1912, the then secretary of the store lived between the grocery and butchery department, once part of the Temperance Hotel. The Society bought 116 Station Road for the then staggering figure of £600, so that it might serve as a permanent secretary's house.

In the early days, the treasurer's job was part-time and was undertaken by a man living at 36 Wansbeck Terrace. When it became a full-time job, the title was changed to 'cashier'. The secretary was always the senior man at the store, the committee feeling that they had no need of a general manager. The president's position remained a part-time one.

From the beginning there was friction between the two Societies concerned with the amalgamation. Which of the two managers was to be manager of Ashington Industrial Co-operative Society? Finally, as a result of this contretemps, there was a breakaway and the Ashington Equitable Society was formed. My great-uncle, Fenwick Barnfather, a check-weigh-man, was the first treasurer (part-time) of the Society. The check-weighman worked at the pit in the weigh cabin. His job was to check the weight of the coal in the tubs. Each tub was marked with the names of the men who had filled it. To ensure that justice was done, the miners employed check-weighmen to check the tubs on their behalf. Although they worked at the pit, they were paid by the miners. Because of this they were not allowed a colliery house, so the miners built houses for them. In

Ashington the check-weighmen's houses were the four houses behind the Miners' Theatre.

In 1912, the AICS had branches at Hirst, Seaton Hirst and Woodhorn. The Equitable Society had its headquarters at Middle Market with a branch at Hirst. This society did not weather the effects of the 1926 strike.

The AICS continued to expand and, in 1924, its splendid new headquarters and shopping arcade were built next to Dungait's Farm, a short distance from the Grand Corner.

The store order man, whose visit I eagerly awaited, carried with him a long, narrow, thin book. I looked for his coming so eagerly because, sometimes, he gave me a piece of carbon paper to play with.

On his first visit, at the beginning of the week, he took the order. On his second, at the end of the week, he collected payment. As he was well aware of the groceries his customers were likely to order, the rhythm he gave to his little recital tended to vary from house to house, the line-endings of his free-verse depending upon his customer's anticipated interruption to give an order.

Flour, salt, sugar,
Tea, coffee, cocoa,
Cigarettes,
Tobacco,
Currants, raisins, lemon-peel, baking powder,
Soap. Toilets.
Soda. Cornflour, rice, ground-rice,
Tapiocasagobarleypepper,
Mustard. Life salts. Starch.
Blue, blacking, black-lead, matches.
Hearthstones.
Yeast, sweets, treacle,
Butter, margarine or lard.
Cheese, ham or bacon.
Peas or beans.
Sauce jam marmalade.
Tinned meat, tinned fruit.

Salmon milk biscuits
Metal polish bun flour scone flour self-raising flour.
Pickles, vinegar, bath-brick.
Anything else?

The store order man with a country round did more than take orders for groceries; he reminded his customers of any possible goods they might need to buy from other departments.

I was once visiting at a fairly isolated cottage when the order man came. After the lady of the house had given her order for food, she said, 'I need a new coat. Well, I don't so much need it as have to get it. Me other one's served for nine years and it could serve for nine years more, but I'm going to a wedding. I fancy a grey one this time. If you wouldn't mind taking me bust measurement. The end of the tape measure's frayed a bit so you'll have to mind to add an inch on. Just send what you think'll suit and ask the lass in the millinery to send a hat to match. I'll give you one of me old ones for size.'

The next week a brown-paper parcel containing a coat and a hat bag with a new hat and her old one inside were delivered with the groceries. They were just what she wanted, she said.

In those days of fairly large family connections and very few telephones, the store order man often delivered verbal messages in an emergency as he went on his rounds. One order man told me that once, just before he was due to set off on a Monday morning, a customer rushed into the shop and asked him if he'd mind delivering a message to her cousin Doris for her. It was that her Uncle Joe had suddenly passed away earlier that morning. Knowing he would have to give all the details to the bereaved relative, he listened carefully to the account of what had happened.

We were in the middle of a heat-wave and already the temperature was beginning to climb, so the order man decided he would deliver his message first and get it off his mind. At the same time he would take Cousin Doris's order and so save himself a trip next day. She lived in one of the outlying cottages, a room and pantry downstairs and two rooms upstairs. It was washing day and, lacking any other facility, she had an enormous pan on the hob. It filled the entire fire space and, in this she was boiling her whites. The poss tub was in the middle of the floor together with a kit full of clothes steeping and various piles of clothes waiting their turn at the tub. On the table was a scrubbing brush, a tin dish containing a pile of washing already scrubbed and waiting its turn in the pan. The room was hot, airless and steamy. She did not expect any company, her family having gone their various ways. Alone, she decided to remove sundry top garments for comfort.

Unsuspecting, the order man came briskly up to the open kitchen door and stretched out his hand preparatory to jingling the sneck (latch) and shouting 'Store' to make his presence known. What he saw through the steam halted him statue-like. The entirely passive and helpless poss tub was being attacked by a much bigger and more animated poss tub made up of large glistening blancmanges, pink and white, as, with concentrated venom, the pink blancmanges wielded a poss-stick, intent on pulverizing whatever came beneath its thudding weight. A white vest did its inadquate best to keep the white blancmanges under control. The pink blancmanges wouldn't be controlled. The supports for this structure were white and bulbous. Th intervening area was covered in navy-blue heck boards (or duck boards), once the property of a granddam and now being 'worn out'.

It took him a little time to recover, but as soon as he could, the order man retired as silently as possible. When he had composed himself, he approached with the maximum amount of noise and coughing, kicking a big stone out of the way, and shouting 'gerraway, there' to a non-existent animal. Then the cry he was waiting for reached his ear.

'Jus taminit. Jus taminit. Whatever you do, don't come in yet.'

When the summons came for him to enter, she looked at him in accusing disbelief.

'It's not Tuesday, is it?' she asked, as though a day had sneaked by without her knowledge while she was engrossed in her quarrel with the poss tub.

'No. No,' he said. 'It's not that. As a matter of fact, I've come to give you a bit of bad news. Your cousin May came running into the shop this morning . . .'

'It's not their Sinclair?'

'No. No. It's your Uncle Joe. He's passed away.'

'Never in the Wide World!'

'Aye. About seven this morning. She was on her way to the undertaker when she called in.'

'But I only saw him on the street last Saturday. He looked all right then. You would have taken a lease on his life.'

'Yes, I know. He went sudden at the finish.'

'Well, I never! I'll have to sit down for a minute. I'm fair knocked out at the news. Did me Cousin May say what happened? How's she taken it? This'll have put paid to her washing.'

'Aye. Well, she said he had a bit of a cold but, like. Nothing much, she thought. He wasn't in much of a fettle, but they didn't think anything of it. Well, she got up to start the washing and she just had the fire going when their Jackie came down to say his granddad wasn't too grand. She went up to see him and she thought he had a right shabby look so she went to make him a cup of tea and give him a powder and when she got back he was lying with his mouth open. It give her an awful gliff, she said. Their Sinclair went for the doctor, but it was too late. Silent pneumonia.'

'Eh, dear. It just goes to show you're never sure. Still, he was living on borrowed time. He passed his three score years and ten a bit back. Ee, well. It was good of you to come. Real good. Can I get you a sup tea?'

'No. Thanks all the same, I'll have to be off. I suppose when I'm here I might as well take your order, if you don't mind.'

'Yes. Just a minute till I get myself collected together. I don't suppose you could pop in and tell our Mary on your way. Tell her I'll be round as soon as I've given Him his dinner.'

Only the main shops had order men. The branch with which we dealt for a time had only the manager and a boy who delivered after school. This shop was square and had two windows dressed with cardboard adverts on stands. The counter on the right, going in, was for serving. The counter set at right angles to this one was split in two to allow access to the back shop. It was used for putting up dry goods. However, the manager rarely had stock ready. Most often, he put up his goods as required. The third counter, exactly opposite the first, was for putting up orders. These were usually delivered singly by the errand boy.

The manager's office was underneath the serving counter. It consisted of the bottom halves of two Woodbine boxes. In one he kept the orders to be put up and, in the other, the orders up and waiting to be paid. I only knew the first box was there because I was once sent to report that our order hadn't been delivered. He got the box out, turned the various pieces of paper over and, sure enough, there was our order stuck to the bottom.

I wouldn't miss going to pay for our order; it was one of the highlights of my week.

Having watched his last customer out of the shop, the manager would place his pencil behind his ear, put both hands on the counter and say, 'Now, hinny?'

'I've come to pay me mother's bill.'

'Right. Now let's see.' And from the shelf below he produced his box and leafed through all the bits of paper there. How I loved this bit. They were all sizes, those bits of paper, most of them torn from anything handy, even the stop-press column of the newspaper. And they were all pencil marks as he'd ticked the items off, and all greasy thumb-prints.

'Here it is,' and he held up my mother's note written in her neat, small script. The paper she had used was never one millimetre larger than was necessary. He put in the prices, turning the paper this way and that to read the writing and holding it up to the light the better to see what had originally been written. When this effort still proved ineffective, he cast his mind back to try to remember what he'd sent. His writing was firm and flowing, the figures being linked to one another by faint loops.

'Right, hinny. That'll be 17s. 8d.'

If this was the amount my mother had given me, I'd hand the money over, wrapped up in paper, and also give him the check book. My mother always sent the correct amount. If the sum didn't agree I'd say, 'That's not what me mother makes it.'

'Isn't it?' he would reply, not in the least put out.

If he got it wrong the second time, I would say, 'It should be 16s. 10d' I wasn't supposed to do this. I was supposed to wait till he had figured it out.

'Ah,' he would say. 'She's right. I can see where I've made my mistake.'

My reward for going this errand was to keep the bill. I kept it with others I had acquired by the same method, and some I'd made up myself, in the bottom half of the Woodbine box and with these I'd play for hours.

One day, I went in and asked for the bill and the manager said, 'How much does your mother make it, pet? (We never called my mother 'Mam' and being a very observant and agreeable sort of man, he saw that we did not and reacted accordingly.)

Caught off guard, I said 'Well, 18s. 2d.'

'That's right,' he said. 'I was looking at her bill a minute ago and I knew you'd be in to pay it, so I did it up.'

As he made out the check I realized I wasn't going to get my booty. The prospective loss sharpened my wits. I took a deep breath.

'Me mother wants the bill,' I said.

He sighed. 'All right, hinny,' he replied and brought out the box, fished around, found what he was looking for and made his calculations so that they tallied with the money I'd given him.

She's right, pet. That's what I make it.

8. Store Funeral

The store order man's encounter with me Cousin Doris brings me rather prematurely to funerals. I was very young indeed when I attended my first funeral. As I cannot remember my brother also being there, I can only assume I was too great a responsibility to be left in someone else's care. I was dressed in my white Sunday dress, my black Sunday shoes, white socks and my Sunday hat. This last item had been denuded of its artificial forget-me-nots and the blue ribbon had been swathed in a black one.

The funeral in question was that of an elderly relative and, naturally they got the store, the funeral arrangements had been handed over to the AICS funeral and joinery department. Bread and cakes were ordered from the bakery, ham from the grocery and tongue from the butchery departments. These last two commodities would be boiled in the set pot.

At this distance in time, all I can give is a series of snapshots from the album of my memory. I recall approaching the house with my mother and father and seeing a great number of men standing round in dark suits and bowler hats. The house door was open and the passage was full of light. It also seemed full of people. The rest of the house was dark because all the curtains were drawn. We made our way along the passage and stopped at the room door. Inside, it also seemed full of people all dressed in black. In the middle of the room was a long wooden box. Underneath it there were a great many flowers.

Somebody said to my parents, 'You'll want to see her before they screw her down.' My mother and father went forward but I stood rooted to the spot. Then the vicar came. He seemed very big and too wide for the passage. Somebody pulled me against the wall. I could hear people crying. It didn't seem right that grown-ups should cry. I heard the vicar mumbling and a terrible thing happened. I started to giggle. I didn't want to giggle. I tried to stop. I bent my head, put my hand over my mouth and squeezed my eyes tightly in an effort to cry, but no tears came. I ground my teeth, but still my shoulders shook. A man put his hand on my shoulder.

'There, there, hinny,' he said. 'Don't take on so.' A shaft of light suddenly made a bright path through the room. 'They're taking her through the window,' the man explained.

Back outside in the sunshine, I stood amazed at the sight. Two big, black horses with plumes on their heads stood in front of the hearse, a long glass box adorned with black knobs and black fancywork. The undertaker, Mr Mallaby, was dressed in a black frockcoat, black trousers, white shirt, stiff white wing collar, black cravat and, making him taller still, a black top-hat. He stood beside the hearse as the underbearers slid the coffin in and then went back for flowers and wreaths to pile on top of it. Then the horses moved forward slightly and Mr Mallaby in a subdued, but very lordly and dignified manner as suited the occasion, called, 'First mourning coach.'

Another pair of black horses drew up pulling a cab. One of Mr

Mallaby's minions went forward, opened the door and let down a step. He stood to attention near the door while Mr Mallaby produced a long sheet of paper and, drawing himself up still further so that he looked even more like a presiding magpie, intoned as though he were introducing royalty, 'Mr and Mrs Andrew Hyslop, daughter and son-in-law erv the deceased. Chief mourners.' There was a pause while my aunt and uncle

. . . erv the deceased

came forward and got into the cab. 'Mr and Mrs William Summers. Eldest son and daughter-in-law erv the deceased.' Only my grandmother made to go into the cab.

'If it's all the same to you,' my grandfather said to Mr Mallaby, 'I'll walk. Let the womenfolk ride.'

This created a precedent. After this, none of my great uncles elected to ride and the cabs, three altogether, were filled with women. They said there was room for me in the last coach and pulled a seat out of nowhere for me to sit on.

'He's packing them in. We'll all be scumfished,' said a woman in black whom I'd never seen before. It turned out she was one of two distant cousins, too distant to be asked to family weddings, but not so distant they couldn't come to funerals. They looked sufficiently red-eyed to appear to be among the near relatives thus, according to Mr Mallaby who had the last word on these occasions, qualifying for two of the places left vacant by my great uncles.

'Mebbe,' the other cousin agreed, a little too tartly for such an occasion, 'but he knows his job. When it comes to funerals, the store takes some beating.'

I kept my eyes on what was happening outside, partly because it was interesting and partly because I didn't like the smell in the cab. It was like nothing I'd ever smelt before. Suddenly – or perhaps gradually, it was difficult for me to tell – everything went still. Then the minute bell began to toll and we moved forward with a jerk. We had to turn two corners, one into Park Road and one at the Catholic church.

From my vantage-point I saw the undertaker setting the slow measured pace, impressive in the garb of his calling. After him came two men carrying a large wreath between them. They were followed by the hearse and behind it the six underbearers. Next followed the three coaches and after them, the long tail of mourners, many of the women carrying flowers. As we gently swayed our slow way to the church, passers-by stood stock-still while the cortège passed, the men having removed their hats.

Even for a hot day, the church was cold and it didn't seem any warmer in the churchyard. My relatives with their solemn faces and black clothes were remote and unlike the people I knew. The gaping mouth of the grave and the dull thud of the earth on the coffin was terrifying. For a while after the vicar had finished speaking, everyone stood looking towards the grave, apparently mesmerized. Then the vicar shook hands with the chief mourners and left. Once more, Mr Mallaby came into his own. He stood among us and everyone gazed at him in respectful silence.

'You are all kindly invited back to tea at the home of the deceased in Park Villas,' he intoned solemnly.

This caused a little stir of activity and a lightening of the air as people hurried (very slowly) away from the graveside, either to walk towards the house or to look at the flowers and wreaths.

My grandfather went up to Mr Mallaby and, as they shook hands, he murmured something about underbearers and whisky.

The relative who had complained about the stuffy cab said to her companion in an undertone, 'Just have a look at who gave all them flowers and see if our Lizzie did send some like she said she was.'

Back at the house, the front room was transformed. It was full of tables and chairs, the latter set out for a meal the like of which I hardly ever saw, even at Christmas.

I still have the mourning card sent to my parents for the funeral. In earlier days mourning cards were not always sent out. Instead, two bidders were appointed.

If the person who died was a woman, two men acted as bidders. Dressed in their best suits, Dobson hats, black arm-bands, black ties and black gloves, they went round to call on the relatives and friends whose names appeared on the list they had been given. Knocking on the door in question, they said, 'You are requested to come to the funeral of Mrs Mary X, number 10 Twelfth Row, gather at two, lift at half-past. Thank you kindly.'

If a man died, two women suitably garbed acted as bidders and, if the deceased was a young person or child, two young people would act as bidders.

Funerals of adults usually took place on Saturday afternoons or Sundays so that the miners who were working could attend without losing a shift. If it was a funeral for a young person, then the wreath-bearers, underbearers and other attendants had to be young – in which case the funeral took place on a Wednesday afternoon so that Mr Mallaby could call on store apprentices to act as functionaries.

In those days, the coffin was taken outside the house and placed on two chairs. While it was there, the vicar came along to say a prayer and a hymn was sung by the mourners. Usually, a good singer was asked to 'lift' the hymn – that is, start it off. One lady in Ashington officiated on occasions like this, both at home and in the church. She was also in demand for lyings-in and layings-out, though her busy schedule did not prevent her from raising her own family. After the funeral, the chief mourners, Mr Mallaby and the underbearers were conveyed in the mourning coaches back to the house where they were each given a glass of whisky. The apprentices didn't get any whisky. Not even dandelion and burdock.

It was seven-and-a-half years before I went to another family funeral, that of my grandmother. Her death was a great shock to us all because we had no prior warning. Shortly after midnight, she simply got up from her chair to go to bed, and died then and there. Incidentally, King George V died later the same day.

On the face of it, my grandmother was like many of her generation. She bore six sons and two daughters, one daughter dying in infancy. Her husband, my grandfather, was a miner. Theirs was a common enough story of pleasure and pain, hard work and some leisure. My grandmother was a staunch Co-operator and an active member of both the Women's Co-operative Guild and the Mothers' Union. Like other houses in the Rows, hers radiated warmth and, whenever possible, laughter and good fellowship.

For my grandmother's funeral the family decided against mourning coaches. From the last house in the first block of the Ninth Row to the church, we walked slowly to the accompaniment of the minute bell. Some of the shops lowered their blinds as the cortège passed and, as they did for other funerals, passersby stood still, the men bare-headed. At the Store Corner, many of the assistants stood silently on the pavement. Members of the Co-operative Guild lined one side of the road leading from the gate to the church door and representatives from the Mothers' Union stood facing them. As we turned towards the church gate, I looked back and saw that the cortège had not yet crossed the road at Portland Corner – it was so long.

Inside the church the choir was already in the choir stalls. It was a very beautiful and most moving service.

The ceremony was, I know, for my grandmother. Nevertheless, in after years I liked to think of its being for all the women who worked as she did, keeping a bright hearth and clean home and as good a table as her economics would allow: women who did this cheerfully but without choice and regardless of the talents they might have had, doomed to a life of providing for others.

You are all kindly invited back to tea

9. Christmas and New Year

For me, the first day of December marked the onset of Christmas. This was because, on the Sunday nearest that date, my grandmother, in the presence of Billy and me, made a little ceremony of taking the clothes basket out from under the bed in the front room and placing in it the first of her Christmas goodies. It might be a box of Chinese figs or a box of dates or sweets. Whatever it was, it had come from the store that week with her order. Each Sunday, till Christmas, we used to visit her, filled with delighted anticipation, to see how the collection had grown during the week. In retrospect, I think this little ceremony was performed solely for our benefit, because the basket she used was known, more prosaically, as the 'dirty basket' for in it was kept the week's accumulation of dirty linen. On Mondays, it was used to hold that same linen washed and ready for ironing. So I think that, during the week, this collection of Christmas fare was kept either in the tall-boys or in the pantry.

She chose the first day of the month because it was then that the store officially recognized the approaching festive season. Any extra temporary staff needed to cope with the additional trade were recruited that week. Thus, even without the ceremony of the basket, I could see from my window that Christmas was almost upon us. Tinsel appeared in the hardware department windows and their normal display of the dull things hardware stores sell – tin bait bottles, brushes, wire netting, irons, shovels, stone hotwater bottles – was replaced by toys, books and games.

It was from these articles on display that we had to make our request to Santa Claus. Like us, he apparently never went past the store. More particularly, he never went past the Ashington Industrial Co-operative Society's Ashington Branch Hardware. There were two sorts of presents – those given to us by friends and relatives and those that came from Santa. So we had to choose what we'd most like and, if we couldn't have that, what we'd like next and so on, for this benevolent man had a mammoth task on his hands. He had to provide for all children from this limited store. The more we got, the less there'd be for others and, inevitably, some would have to go without. Also, he might consider our first choice inappropriate. In his omniscience he might think it better that our first choice went to some other child and, like the judges of newspaper competitions, his decision was final and he entered into no correspondence on the subject. Thus we made second, third and even fourth choices.

Only once did we defect from Ashington hardware. The headquarters of the AICS were at Hirst and the hardware department there opened up one of the upstairs rooms for the three of four weeks prior to Christmas. This was, in effect, a restrained toy fair. One Christmas we were taken there by both my father and mother. My father's being there was most unusual; he rarely went shopping. We were asked to make the usual choices from the goods on display.

There were drawbacks to this system. First of all, the expedition took place only two days before Christmas when the stock was probably depleted; secondly, we were asked to choose from toys many of which we had not seen before. At the other shop we had days and days to look at its display, time to weigh up what was there, time to make up our minds and change them many times. Here we had to make an irrevocable decision in a short time. The following year we returned to Ashington hardware and there we continued, steadfast in our loyalty, till the end of my school life when we were well past the toy stage and the things we wanted (mostly books) were ordered from there.

Except at Christmas, we rarely shopped in the greengrocery department because, apart from the large gardens that went with our house, my father had a double allotment. With both my parents being keen and successful gardeners, we had an abundant supply of potatoes and vegetables of all sorts throughout the year.

By Christmas Day, my grandmother's basket was full (or so it seemed) and we all went to her house for the day. It was very like a Sunday, only more so. At meal-times, my grandfather and all the men sat at the kitchen table, the women sat at the round table in the front room and we children sat at the settle. Sometimes my grandfather got a small barrel of beer in for Christmas, sometimes bottles. There was always beer to drink with the Christmas dinner, with shandy for those of my aunts who could be persuaded to sample this drink, dandelion and burdock for those who could not, and lemonade for us children. My grandfather, along with the other men, had his Yorkshire Pudding before his dinner as usual. The women and children had theirs with their meal.

All the food was served from the oven door and the fender, this last protected by newspaper. The women supervised the food that went on to their spouses' plates. My mother would say: 'That's enough meat for Archie and only a little spoonful of turnip. He likes it, but it doesn't like him. And just put the gravy on his potatoes.' Then Auntie Anna would join: 'Give Kit a little bit more crackling. He can have mine. I'm not that fond of it. He mebbe shouldn't eat it, but it's Christmas.'

Naturally, tea was augmented by the iced Christmas cake. My grandmother made one; in our house, we had two – a little one and a big one. The little one was a trial to see if the big one was good enough. The big cake was very special and only eaten freely at Christmas and New year, after which it was kept for visitors and special occasions and was expected to last until the following December. The making of the Christmas cake was a very important undertaking with my mother, but not as important as it was to my Aunts Ethel, Isa and Amy at Wooler. Their cakes were made in the summer in time for the Wooler Show. If they weren't satisfied with the first, they made a second. Their cakes were of such excellence they won many prizes at each succeeding show. To improve on perfection, they added special ingredients of their own. To me, as a child, this was a solemn ritual, at which I was, naturally, only a spectator.

'Now, Margaret, I have something to show you,' and out came the cake, rich brown in colour and perfect in texture.

'It's delicious. Really lovely.'

'Yes. But what's in it?'

'Well, now. Let me taste. Oh, Be Joyful.'

'Ye–es.'

'Um. A different sort of fruit. Or nuts?'

'Ye–es.'

'And, there is a something . . . I'm not quite sure . . .' Even today, Auntie Isa makes my Christmas cake.

In spite of the delicacies added to the normal fare, my grandfather still had to resort to meat sandwiches. Sucking out the various bits of chocolate log cake, mince pies, trifle, etc., from between his teeth, he'd say how fancy cakes were all right for womenfolk, but they were hardly likely to fill a man up.

At night, most of the adults played New Market while we read our Christmas books.

I remember Christmas 1928. I desperately wanted a Fairy bike – a small child's two-wheeler. My nightly prayers ended with, 'and please God let me get a Fairy bike for Christmas.' In church I constantly reminded God not to forget. I worked hard at school. I ran errands and helped at home. I left nothing to chance. On Christmas morning, hanging from the bed-rail, was my stocking, the contents of which were the same as Billy's, one penny, an apple, an orange and some figs, nuts, dates and grapes each done up in small screws of paper. Other than that we each got a Big Story Book (big in size and lettering, but small in content) a game and a toy. My game was a set of draughts, my toy, a post office set. Neither Santa nor God, it seemed, thought a Fairy bike would be good for me. Later in the day our finances were added to till we had tenpence each.

We also had parties to attend. For the Sunday School party we each took our own cups and some scones or cake to grace the table. As we left to go home, we each got a gift. There were probably prizes for those who won games, but, if this was so, I did not win any.

Then the Co-op Women's Guild would organize a Christmas party for the children. Each member was allowed to send one child. As both my mother and my grandmother were members, my brother and I were both able to go. The meal was provided free, I think, and was followed by games – or, rather, the programme said there would be games but these were very difficult to get off the ground. The party I remember most clearly was held in the large hall above the store's various departments. It had a raised platform at one end and here stood the piano. During the meal we all had to be quiet and restrained. We were asked to sit quietly against the wall after the meal was over, while the tables were being cleared. Perhaps we did for two minutes or so. By the time the room was ready for games, however, we had become a noisy host of ceaseless activity intent or running up and down the room, on to the platform and off it. Finally, one brave child lifted the lid of the piano and tested the keyboard. Immediately, the instrument was thronged with children. We swarmed over it. Those who could get near thumped the keys; those who could not added their quota of sound by banging the lid on top of the piano up and down. It was extremely difficult for the good ladies to regain order. It was impossible for them to tell any child off lest they give offence to one of their members. The best thing they could do in the circumstances was the Grand Old Duke of York with the more manageable of the party-goers.

When it was time to go home, we each got an apple or an orange and a bar of toffee. This was CWS toffee which I never saw on sale. It was hard. You couldn't break it or chew it; it had to be sucked. So you peeled the paper halfway down in order to give yourself something to hang on to, and started to lick. Soon everything in sight was sticky. It had excellent lasting properties. With care, I have no doubt, it could have been licked till tongue fatigue set in, put to one side and taken up at intervals to last through the holidays.

The Guild also gave a dinner to its members. The cost of this was 1s.6d. (7½p), 6d. (2½p) of which was paid out of the Guild funds.

When Christmas was over, we began to prepare for New Year. My parents were tee-total but that did not mean we kept no spirits or ale in the house. We always kept both whisky and brandy, but this was for their medicinal qualities only. Whisky was extremely efficacious for adults who had a cold, but it was a remedy few adults would dream of taking on their own initiative. After the victim had appeared with a red nose, or coughed and sneezed a bit, someone with medical authority (a neighbour or relation) would say, 'What you want is a good stiff dose of whisky. Now, don't look at me as if I didn't know what I was talking about. Listen. Get yourself away back home and put that much whisky' – indicating a generous measure between thumb and forefinger – 'into a tumbler. Add a little bit of hot water, not very much, and a little bit of sugar. Drink it and get into bed and sweat that cold out of your system. It'll do you a power of good, mark my words.'

The sufferer often had to take this medicine for several nights before recovery was total, and then the praise would be fulsome. 'I had this terrible cold. Couldn't get me breath. Pains in me chest. Me nose wouldn't stop running and cough! You never heard anything like it! Then somebody told me just to take a sup whisky in a bit of hot water. You wouldn't believe the good it did me. I tell you what it is, if it hadn't been for that whisky, I would have had pneumonia.'

At New Year, the whisky was transferred, metaphorically, from the medicine chest to the sideboard ready for the First Foot or any distinguished reveller.

Not so the brandy. This was for all ailments other than colds and to emphasize its medicinal role, it was always administered on a teaspoon.

Not many years ago I met an elderly friend I had not seen in ages. I asked after her health. 'Oh, I'm all right,' she said. 'Nothing ever ails me. But me sister has been shabby. Real shabby. At one time we thought we might lose her. Congestion of the lungs. Night and day I sat with her and not a bite could she eat. Every now and then, it was all I could do to get a teaspoonful of brandy past her lips, but, you see, it pulled her through.'

'Didn't the doctor prescribe antibiotics?' I asked.

'Doctor! Oh, we didn't bother the doctor. She would have been terribly upset if she thought we'd bothered the doctor.'

To complement the whisky we had a bottle of port and some bottles of ginger wine made from a fourpenny bottle of ginger wine essence. These came from the store chemist as did a bottle of Australian wine costing 3s.6d. (17½p), which, for some reason, was purchased one year to add to the board. The shortbread Auntie Nan sent from Edinburgh was kept for New Year and thick and rich and delicious it was. Because we lived so near the Border, we had a perk: we celebrated Christmas in the English fashion and New Year in the Scottish style.

For health reasons, my parents made (and drank) Dr Watson's Tonic Stout from a sixpenny packet of the same name. This beverage was mixed in the huge bread-baking dish and while it was being made, the scullery became a brewery. Bottled, the resultant concoction was stored behind the wardrobe in my room. One night, we awoke with an awful start. We thought our house had been invaded and somebody with a machine-gun was intent on murdering us in our beds. When light was finally available, we saw that dark-brown streams and rivulets of Dr Watson's curative beverage had burst from their bottles and were splattered on the ceiling and down the walls. Dr Watson had to do without our custom after that.

At this season of the year, we made official visits to members of the family we visited as a matter of course throughout the year. The word 'babysitter' had not then been coined, nor would my parents have had much use for them had they existed. When they were asked out to tea or supper, we went too. Among those we visited frequently were Aunt Martha and Uncle Tommy. They were really my father's uncle and aunt and they lived in Council Terrace. They had no children, their only child, Hilda, having died tragically of diphtheria when she was six years old. But they did have a dog, Lady.

Aunt Martha's house was always spotlessly clean and the mat in her scullery would not have disgraced a front room. The living-room had a dining table with a plush cloth, four horse-hair dining chairs, a horse-hair sofa and a press, as well as the usual cupboards and kitchen range. On the mantelshelf was a pair of brass candlesticks, a pair of brass shoes, a clock, china ornaments of Prince Albert and Queen Victoria, and a mug commemorating the marriage of George V and Queen Mary. Above these was a dark-blue glass rolling pin suspended by a gold cord. There was a message in gold writing saying, 'A Present from Bournemouth'. On the side were pictures of cherubs looking heavenward and clinging to a cross. The mat in front of the fire was black with red loops and whirls and the tablecloth had fringes. Sometimes I counted 80, sometimes 78. The sofa scratched the backs of your legs. There was nothing to read but *Sunday Stories* and *The Methodist Weekly*.

When we visited on a weekday we went to the back door, but, on Sundays and Christmas, we went to the front door and sat in the front room. It had a marble fireplace with brass fender and fire irons, an over-mantel laden with the best glass ornaments and, down the sides, there were long glass panels with bull-rushes painted down the edges. In the summer it wasn't always possible to see exactly what was in the room because the curtains were drawn in case the carpet got faded. Where you could see it – and not very much was exposed to the destructive rays of the sun – the carpet was dark green with flowers. The horse-hair sofa was very much higher and harder than the other one and it had a fur animal skin draped across the back. On the wall was a huge picture of Uncle Tommy, Aunt Martha and Hilda. Hilda had long, fair, wavy hair and she was dressed in white with broderie anglais trimming, white socks and white kid slippers. Everywhere else there were little tables, while the sideboard supported numerous photgraphs in frames and dangling crystal ornaments.

We always ate in the kitchen, usually roast lean ham, pease pudding and chutney, all home-made. There were tarts, teacakes and cakes to follow, but my aunt and uncle were exceptionally fond of caraway seeds and everything which could be flavoured with caraway was. This severely limited what we ate because we were not allowed to remove the seeds and leave them on our plates. Lady was very fond of ham, pease pudding, chutney and caraway seeds. She sat next to Uncle Tommy at table and they went shares with whatever was on Uncle Tommy's plate, one forkful for Uncle Tommy, one forkful for Lady. As table manners go, Lady's were impeccable, although she didn't actually bound with life at the best of times. She had no interest in us at all and our coming rarely disturbed her slumbers in front of the fire. She didn't go to chapel or to the pit, but, other than that, she went everywhere with Uncle Tommy, who was a great talker and thus she became patient, not to say apathetic.

One night after Uncle Tommy had arrived from the pit, had his bath and his meal, he decided to take the dog for a walk and call in at our house. He was on late shift so it was almost ten o'clock by the time he got to our place. My parents were just thinking of going to bed because my father was 'in first' and started at 6am. Lady fell asleep, my mother did her best to stay awake and, finally, at half-past five, Uncle Tommy decided to set my father down to the telephone exchange before he, Uncle Tommy, went to bed.

On another occasion he set out to see the Northumberland Plate, a race he'd heard much about but never seen. What with stopping to chat with this one and that when he left the pit, missing the train, getting on the wrong bus and asking the tram driver how his vehicle operated, he arrived at the course when they were tidying up the rubbish at the end of the day.

Aunt Martha and Uncle Tommy were extremely kind to us. When I said that I'd never been to Newcastle to see the shops at Christmas, Aunt Martha said she would take me. When we got home, my mother was annoyed, saying that my making the remark had obliged Aunt Martha to make her offer. I went determined not to make a nuisance of myself and to be properly grateful for the experience. We went first to the market where I admired everything on display regardless, particularly a small pink manicure set, the garish colour of which had caught my eye. And of all the useless things, a manicure set. It was priced sixpence. You could get marvellous pencil cases for that price at Woolworth's in Ashington. Nevertheless, I admired it.

'Do you really like it?' Aunt Martha asked.

'Oh, yes. It's beautiful.'

'I can't see it being that much use, but if you like it so much that's all that matters. Would you like it for your Christmas present?'

So there it was. One present the less to be surprised by. She must have found my tireless appreciation and fulsome thanks very trying.

It was at Christmas and New Year that 'the guisers' came round. The word probably derives from 'disguise' because those concerned dressed up in anything that took their fancy, even blackening their faces with soot or boot polish if they thought it would produce a better effect. Their function was to amuse but, first, they asked permission to enter.

'Please will you let the guisers in?'

After that they generally did a playlet handed down by word of mouth for generations and involving the presence of Saint George, a fight with makeshift swords, a death and the calling of Doctor Brown, the best old Doctor in the town

When the latter was asked what he could cure, he answered, 'A dead man, to be sure,' and, thereafter, breathed life back into the corpse who sat up and sang:

Once I was dead, now I'm alive.
God Bless the doctor that made me survive.
A pocket full of money and a bellyful of beer,
I wish you a Merry Christmas and a Happy New Year.
The roads are very clarty, me boots are very thin,
I've got a little money box to keep me money in.

After this gentle hint, one of the guisers went round rattling the box for a contribution before they left amid laughter and mutual good wishes.

The money Billy and I were given for Christmas was not to spend. A far worthier end awaited it. My mother was a staunch disciple of the Micawber principle 'annual income £1 – annual expenditure 19s.6d – result – happiness'. Thus we were given a Saturday penny which could be squandered on sweets. And that was the total allowance of what we could so spend. Anything else had to go into the 'thrifty' – a red tin postbox which, one for my brother and one for me, stood on the top shelf of the cupboard. I must confess that in the matter of sweets, I did go past the store. After much thought and much gazing in sweet-shop windows, my penny was finally disposed of where I felt I could get most value for money. I held on to my money, changing it into as many different denominations as I could – twenty half-pennies, sixpence and four pennies, etc., etc. – till I drove everyone mad and I was commanded to feed it into the wide-grinned victorious mouth of the postbox. The next Saturday, I either took it myself, or it was taken for me, together with my bank book, to the Store Penny Bank in the Hirst Arcade. Every Saturday this excursion was made. Most weeks we put in threepence each, but, occasionally, we took the bank at its word and deposited a single penny.

10. The Guild

The Co-operative Women's Guild began in June 1883 as the Women's League for the Spread of Co-operation. They were active women who believed in Co-operation but who were disenchanted with its administration, for the movement was almost entirely run by men; the women, without whose help no society could exist, were useful only for their 'basket power'.

It was the women who, in almost all cases, had to eke out what were sometimes very small wages so that the needs of the family could be met. The quality of goods the store sold were beyond doubt excellent and the dividend they gave welcome and useful, but these facts often militated against membership and loyalty to the Co-op. The very poor just could not afford to deal at the store. The eventual bonus of 3s.(15p) or 2s. 6d. (12½p) in the pound dividend was not a sufficient inducement for them to buy goods which could be bought cheaper elsewhere. The Guild existed to try to bring these facts, and others, home to committeemen and those who directed a Society's policy.

In addition, although it was the women who did the shopping and paid the household bills, it was the man of the house who was the member and who had the vote. Thus, the women of the Guild campaigned for open membership. My mother was a very vocal advocate (among the family) for the women as well as the men to be members of the store and, in this way, she prevailed upon several to 'join the store' in their own right.

Each week at the Guild meeting there would be a speaker whose topic usually had some relevance to women as citizens. In the early days there had been very few women officiating in the Co-op and, in spite of the hard work done by the Guild members, these numbers increased very little as the years passed. The only photograph I have of Ashington Board of Management was taken in the 1930s. Its members are all male. Thumbing through old Co-op publications, one definitely gets the impression that the movement as a whole was completely male-dominated. Pictures of directors, managers, Co-operators in all administrative walks of life proliferate; all show men.

Yet since before 1896 the Guild was active in taking up issues that affected the lives of all Co-operators, men and women and their families. In 1896 it made an inquiry into the wages and conditions of Co-op employees, and in 1902 investigated relations between the poor and the Co-op. In 1914 it appalled the dignitaries of the church by campaigning for divorce reform.

The Co-operative Women's Guild held an annual conference which was attended by women from all over the world, including the USA and Russia. Recommendations covered wide-ranging issues: it was proposed that a study of Esperanto be made for international purposes, that there should be a cessation of competition in armaments, that the manufacture of poison gas be abolished, that there should be an increase in the old-age pensions commensurate with the cost of living and that any worker over 60 should qualify as a recipient, and that more and better houses should be built by local authorities. Guild members fought for the enfranchisement of women, pledged themselves to fight for peace and co-operation, campaigned for a Co-operative daily newspaper, called for a reduction in working hours and the establishment of a 40-hour week, petitioned for the inclusion of agricultural and domestic workers in unemployment insurance, asked for the raising of the school-leaving age and appealed for better welfare for mothers after childbirth and clinics for women of 40 and over.

They saw the Co-operative movement not simply as a form of trading for mutual benefit but as a principle to be applied to all human affairs and relationships, in order to achieve a decent and improved standard of life for everyone – not only in Britain, but all the world over. A Co-operative way of life, they thought, would make for friendly and satisfactory relationships with people in other lands as well as those who lived in different parts of the United Kingdom. Peace and prosperity at home and abroad would follow in the wake of Co-operation properly practised. Women, it was felt, had an important part to play in realizing this Utopia and hence their voices should be heard and listened to.

The women of Ashington Guild were sincere in their beliefs and animated in their vision. When they sang 'Pull Down the Wretched Cottages' you had the feeling they were going to pull them down there and then, in spite of the fact they had done a week's wash. And when they sang 'Oh Happy Band of Pilgrims' they looked happy. If they hadn't achieved anything today, they might tomorrow.

The women were different beings here in the meeting. I do not think my grandfather ever thought of my grandmother's going to the Guild as anything other than a legitimate night out to allow her to have a bit of a gossip with other womenfolk. In her turn, she was a valued member of the Guild, but she did not see that her aspirations there were at variance with her practice at home.

And for all the energy generated at these meetings, I still asked myself one question: why, I wondered, did they sing 'brother clasps the hands of brother, stepping fearless through the night'? Why not sister clasps the hands of sister?

11. The Co-op News

The only papers we took regularly at home were the *Manchester Guardian*, together with *John O'London's Weekly* and *John Bull*. I regret to have to admit that I found this reading matter very dull and much preferred the papers favoured by my grandparents. These were the *News of the World*, *Reynolds News* (a Co-op publication) and *Thomson's Weekly News*. After Sunday School I used to slip quietly into their house, slide on to the end of the form and read what was to be found on the paper rack that hung on the wall near the window. The newest paper was at the top and the oldest the one due for its last destination 'across the road', at the bottom.

In the silence I kept myself up to date with the bizarre world 'down South'. Thus I stayed engrossed till my grandparents and uncles, who had been sleeping off the effects of Sunday dinner, should rouse themselves, refreshed and ready for Sunday tea.

They did take one other periodical regularly. This was the *Co-operative News* and it was taken specifically for my grandfather. Honesty compels me to reveal he never read a word of it. My grandfather was a shot-firer. He liked the '*Co-op News*' for making his shots: the page was just the right size and the paper the right weight.

*My Grandfather, Bill Summers: a master cutter-man
– one of the first*

Like the wise virgins, he kept his lamp clean, trim and ready for use always. After the meal was over, the table cleared and the dishes washed and, most important, the table rubbed down, he prepared to clean his lamp. When this was done, he filled the bottom part of the lamp with carbide and the top with water. With his hand, he scooped up any carbide remaining on the table and returned it to the bag from which it had come.

Then he made his shots. He tore the *News* up into single sheets. Then taking a thinnish circular piece of wood which he kept for the purpose, and beginning at one corner of the paper, he carefully rolled it round the wood, after which he twisted one end of the paper and extracted the wood. He filled this empty tube of paper with gunpowder, dadding it down for the powder (or 'poother', as it was known) to settle. When the tube was nearly full, he twisted the other end and his shot was ready.

Both gunpowder and carbide were kept in the pantry; the

gunpowder in a jar on the floor beside the pails of water and the carbide on the top shelf.

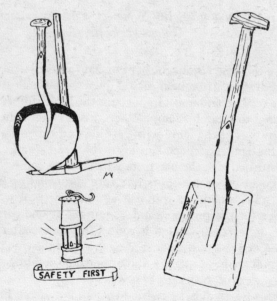

ACC shovel – still in use!

12. The Store Half-Year and the CWS

Headquarters, Ashington Industrial Co-operative Society

Self-denial Week for the store lasted much longer than seven days. We tightened our belts, metaphorically speaking, for upwards of three weeks or a month. These Lenten Days came twice a year and were otherwise known as 'the end of the store half-year'. These were the days, two of them, when all accounts had to be settled. Failure to settle your debts might mean that your name was put on the Black List.

Most provident housewives tried to ensure that their bills would be paid by taking out clubs. These clubs were paid weekly, usually on the grocery order. Each club was worth £1 and was paid over 20 weeks at the rate of 1s. (5p) a week. Each group of 20 clubs was put in a hat and numbers drawn. Whoever got number one could spend her pound straightaway as the first shilling had already been paid. Number two had to wait till the second week and so on. Those with what they called 'backerly lots' had to wait till the club was paid up or almost paid up. So that having a club, or clubs, due immediately before the store half-year was fortunate indeed. Most bills were due in the drapery and hardware departments. The grocery department tended to see that its balances (the amount left over when the customer had paid what she could afford that week) did not get out of hand. Nevertheless, other departments suffered in this lean time, notably the butchery and the grocery. Orders were cut to a minimum and meat was replaced by sausage, mince or corned beef, or done without altogether.

We had two check books in our house. My father's number was 5905 and my mother's 9271. My mother kept a vigilant eye on them to ensure there was an equal amount on both books and that they were made up to a pound. Dividend was paid to the nearest pound. As the dividend could be as high as 2s. 6d. (12½p) in the pound, it made sense to see that, if possible, your purchases came to round figures. On one occasion I was sent to the grocery just before the shop closed on the last day of a half-year for a quarter of butter and the request, 'Twopence on this book, please, and twopence halfpenny on that.' I can see the man's face yet as I spoke.

All departments, except those selling food and chemist's goods, closed for two days for stock-taking at the end of the half-year. When they reopened it was for the 'Half-year End Sale'. These were genuine sales when real bargains were to be had. I cannot speak for other families, but, during my childhood, all our underwear, at least, was bought at these sales. By the time the departments which had closed their doors opened them again on the first morning after stock-taking, there were sizeable queues waiting and every housewife there would have finished her considerable housework before she left home. After the wear and tear of shopping among the crowds in the various departments in which she was interested, she would go home laden with brown-paper parcels, probably give her returning family a 'put off' meal and then return to the store for the afternoon.

I have before me a list of articles bought from the 1927 winter sale.

	£. s. d.	Decimal equivalent
2 boys' shirts @ 1/9½ ea.	3.7	18½
Pillow cotton	4.0	20
1 pr boys' short trousers	2.11	14½
10 yds curtain net @ 1/3 per yd	12.6	62½
2 towels @ 8½d ea.	1.11	9½
1 tablecloth	1.11	9½
2 yds felting @ 1/7 pr yd	3.4	17
2 prs boys' combs. @ 1/9 ea.	3.6	18
2 men's shirts @ 10/2 ea.	1.0.4	1.02
3 prs men's socks @ 1/11½ ea.	3.11	19½
2 body shirts @ 1/4½ ea.	2.9	11
2 prs linings @ 1/9	3.6	18
2 boys' shirts @ 2/9	5.6	27½
2 prs girls' combs. @ 1/3	2.6	12½
2 prs girls' knickers @ 1/3	2.6	12½
1 liberty bodice	1.9	9
2 ladies' vest @ 1/9 ea.	3.6	18
1 pr corsets	3.11	19
	£4.3.4	£4.13½

These would be quality goods sold at reduced prices. It was possible to get goods cheaper than these because I remember one drapery employee telling me at a sale time about a customer of *very* outsize girth holding up a vest, the cost of which was 9d (3½p) and saying, 'Hinny, is there anywhere where I can try this on?'

Not only was there a half-year to pay for these things, there was the dividend yet to be declared. This fluctuated between, I think, 2s. 6d. (12½p) and 2s. (10p) in the pound. One of my aunts considered this to be quite low. Their dividend was usually

3s. 6d. (17½p) in the pound. However, my parents were very satisfied with what they got. My mother never used the dividend to help pay her accounts; it went straight on to hers and father's passbooks.

I am told by my uncle (who worked in the store) that during the 1926 strike all store members were given credit. Some of the bills were quite high as the strike neared its end. He also tells me that the officials of the store met with the Ashington mine owners and asked if the sums owing them could be deducted regularly from the miners' wages at source when the pits started up again. The mine owners could not accede to this request and tick from the AICS at least had to be stopped or slowed down considerably. Officially, members were allowed eight weeks' credit, but it was left to the individual manager's discretion.

Once the AICS stopped giving credit, the 'Equitable' Store started to give credit. During the strike, many of their employees worked overtime for nothing, expecting to be paid when their growing membership went back to work. Alas! When the pits did start again, these new customers forgot their promises of allegiance and deserted the Equitable. Debts to be paid were slow in coming in, even by instalments and, as a result, this store went into liquidation. When the strike was over, debts to the AICS had to be paid back at the rate of 2s. (10p) per week. Some, however, could not afford this amount and, I think that, for them, the weekly payment was reduced sometimes to as little as 3d. (1p) per week. Some, I am told, were still paying off when the Second World War started.

All my father's suits and my mother's coats and costumes (suits) were made to measure at the bespoke tailoring. A great many more clothes were made to measure then than now. The bespoke department effaced itself as much as possible. You had to be intent on finding it to see it at all. It was situated in the dark at the top of the stairs that led to the warren of rooms over the hardware and grocery departments. It was to the left. There was so much material in the crowded room that it appeared as dark inside as it was on the landing.

When the decision had been made to 'go to the tailor's', my mother went for the pattern books. Much time and effort went into choosing a suitable material. When the choice was finally made, if it was a suit for my father, he had, perforce, to go to the department himself. This was one area of shopping that could not be done for him. The tailor took his measurements, and three fittings followed at intervals, the last for the completed garments.

For the rest, my mother chose all my father's socks, shirts and ties. (In winter he wore handknitted socks). Anything else he needed was brought 'on appro' from the store in order for him to make his choice in the privacy of his home. As many as four pairs of boots would arrive 'on appro'. The same would go for other things, too. Even for personal shopping, it was fairly common for a customer to say, 'I'll take that pair, that pair and that pair on appro,' even if it was only bedroom slippers. Outdoor clothes and dresses would go through a similar process. Apart from my confirmation dress, all my dresses were made at home till I left school, after which a large proportion were 'dress-maker made'.

Any large items we bought, such as furniture, were purchased from the CWS premises in Newcastle. To go there, you had first to get a note from your own store or Society. This outing was an event that ate up the entire day.

The CWS drapery premises were huge and elegant, six storeys high. There was a great deal of space in which to display merchandise. When goods were purchased, they were sent to the customers via their society. I think the dividend on these purchases was slightly higher than that given by the Society.

One such article we got by this method was, I remember, absolutely the latest thing (or so we were told) in radiograms. It was a cabinet model. The lid lifted up and underneath was the gramophone part. On one side was the turntable on which six records could be played one after the other without their having to be changed. On the other side was a box arrangement in which to keep the records. The front of the cabinet was divided into four sections by two rows of buttons, one running vertically, the other horizontally. The bottom-right quarter housed the speaker and the bottom left, a large glass-fronted dial with a pointer. Round the dial, the whole world was spread: Tokyo, Oslo, Moscow, Rio de Janeiro, New York, Darjeeling, New Orleans, Durban, etc. – anywhere you cared to name. These names were

CWS drapery, Newcastle-upon-Tyne

repeated on the buttons. All you had to do was press the button for the station of your choice and, with banshee wails and cracklings of rheumatic bones, the genie of the 'gram whizzed off and the pointer on the dial spun round and halted. A high-pitched gabble was discernible above the other noises. You were there. That's how they talked in Tokyo or wherever else you'd tuned in to. Most often what you got was a faint trace of melody being played on an old violin, a little out of tune. This, we supposed, was what passed for music in far-off foreign parts.

Only one button had no destination written on its little round dial.

'What's that for?' we asked.

'That,' said the man who'd come to set up the 'gram weightily, 'is for television.'

We were impressed beyond measure. We'd heard of television but vaguely. It was one of the marvels belonging to the future. We had no real idea of what it was.

'When it comes,' said the man, 'all you will have to do is press that button and there it will be – television.'

We didn't like to parade our ignorance and ask what exactly would happen, which was just as well. Later, increased knowledge led us to suppose his understanding of television was no better than ours.

After a month or so of button-pressing and frantic pointer activity for the benefit of anyone who'd come to see this marvel, we finally set the instrument for the Home Service and there it remained till its demise.

13. Store Classes

'Our story opens very sadly . . . but it is necessary that you should know something about those dark days, just before the sun of Co-operation arose and pushed aside the heaviest clouds that ever hung over England and its people.'

Thus began chapter 1 of *'Our Story: A History of the Co-operative Movement for Young Co-operators* by Isa Nicholson. I had started the store classes. I was nine years of age on the day I first walked up those wooden stairs to start my first class.

We met in a smallish room leading off from the main hall, but also accessible from the landing. In the first part of the class we worked systematically through *Our Story* and, in the second, we played games. We were given homework and at the end of the spring term there were examinations. The course in its entirety dealt with the history of the Co-operative movement generally and with the lives and works of the early philanthropists who paved the way for the movement and who often started Co-operatives themselves, but these Co-operatives failed. Our revered founders, the Rochdale Pioneers, were the men who got it right.

My notebooks from this period, which I still have, lie between covers emblazoned with Co-operative sayings:

Self-help Not Selfish Help Is What We Seek
Each For All And All For Each
Learn To Labour And To Wait

From these books I see that in the 1930s the membership of the AICS was 10,984, the share capital £209,322 and that 5 per cent interest was paid on share capital. Profits were shared in accordance with money spent and the dividend for one particular quarter was 1s. 6d. (7½p) in the pound. I see that I have omitted to mention the dairy and jewellery departments and the café. The dairy department was situated near the station and the jewellery and café in the arcade. In my childhood I had no cause to visit any of these, hence the omission.

I also see that, on the death of a member, money was paid to his wife or a relative according to the amount of purchases the deceased had made over past years.

The work of the education committee (of which my uncle was a member) was to arrange classes for juniors and adults, lectures, concerts, junior choir and orchestra, library, weekend schools, etc. I don't know what the 'etc.' stood for.

I find that one of the questions I had to answer was: 'Imagine you are in a strange village where there was no Co-op. How would you set about establishing one and what would be your reasons?' This question would probably come from the Stage Three examinations.

I note that I have written down the questions asked at at least two examinations immediately after the session was over. I am surprised at their depth. I had always imagined the work was easy. However, with hindsight, I don't think it was so easy after all, because I remember working very hard beforehand. The word I should have remembered was not 'easy' but 'interesting'.

I see the questions for one examination covered the life and work of Robert Owen, Co-operative papers, dividend, loyalty, CWS warehouses, our own store and the work of children in mines, mills and factories. Another had questions covering changes made in the lives of the people by the introduction of machinery in factories, Robert Owen's model village, the work of Lord Shaftesbury, the Rochdale Pioneers, the difference between production and distribution, the CWS, the benefits of Co-operation, factories making CWS goods, reasons for the emblem and motto of the movement, the real meaning of Co-operation and why so many attempts to found a Co-operative failed.

Some weeks later the results of the examinations were published in the *Wheatsheaf*, another Co-operative periodical. Then we had a sports day when we ran races for prizes, had tea (buns and lemonade) and then assembled for prize-giving. All of this was free to regular attenders.

In my first examination, I see from my notebook, I was second in the Stage One examination with 77 per cent. For this, I received three books *Theresa's First Term, House of the Golden Hind* and *Bunch, a Brownie*. The following year I was again second with 80 per cent and was given *The Dorothea Moore Omnibus, The New Prefect* and *The New Girl*.

Before the examination results of Stage Three were published we had a visit from the education secretary. I was at the grammar (or secondary) school by this time and had just discovered poetry. Also, having a fair amount of school work to do at that time, I had learned to write with speed. I do remember filling a second answer book in the Stage Three examination.

Apparently, I had started and ended each answer with a few lines from a poem. Besides taking up the examiner's time needlessly, 'Swiftly walk over the western wave, Spirit of Night' was not a suitable beginning for an answer to a question on the dark days before the advent of Co-operation, the education secretary admonished, nor 'Much have I travelled in the realms of gold' a relevant coda to the success of the Rochdale Pioneers' venture. Nor did Robert Owen 'look up to a dark blue velvet sky studded with silver stars' when he had his inspiration about what a factory owner should really do for his work-people. These and many other misdeeds had I committed, not to mention that my writing towards the end was almost unreadable. My father tut-tutted in agreement with the venerable secretary's words which I thought rather base, because, when writing, my father rarely used a one-syllable word if a five-syllable word would suffice. Thoroughly demoralized, I was completely bewildered when the secretary informed me I had been placed top with 96 per cent. I couldn't get rid of the feeling that some other child who had covered only one page in beautiful script had come first. Anyway, from that examination I was awarded *Little Women* and *Good Wives*, another £10-worth of books and a scholarship.

The reason I was awarded more than one prize was because those placed first, second and third in local examinations had their papers sent for re-examination on an area basis and, from there, top papers were marked on a national basis. I think the top five in area and national placings got prizes. In Stage Three I got the area (£10) and national (scholarship) awards.

Actually, I won two scholarships that year and I was allowed to take them in successive years. The other was from our own society. Each year there were six scholarships – two junior, two senior and two adult. My brother also won one of the junior scholarships in his day.

These scholarships were Summer School Scholarships tenable for one week at one of the establishments taken for the purpose. All expenses were paid. All you had to find was pocket money.

How can I describe those holidays! The vocabulary at my command seems so limited. I already considered myself to be more fortunate than most because, together with some of our cousins, my brother and I spent some of our holidays at Wooler or Edinburgh. These I had always enjoyed.

But this was something else. To begin with, there was the travelling. I and another girl travelled unaccompanied from Newcastle to Southport. Those weeks of preparation. Excitement mounting as the days passed! *Three* new dresses. New sandals. Extra new tennis socks. Chocolate, biscuits and sandwiches to eat on the journey – the things I'd asked for, not the things that were good for me. No Columbus setting out for America prepared for a more exciting journey.

Eventually, I was ready and I was given 10s. (50p) to spend. Ten shillings to spend on myself in one week! I had 2s. 6d. (12½p) in change in my purse and three halfcrowns placed for safety in a little home-made calico bag and sewn inside my vest.

The wonder and joy of that first early-evening walk, boys and girls together. Even today the sight and smell of flowering privet on a summer's evening can send me back to those moments and I feel again the soft, spring tread of new crêpe-soled sandals, the smooth caress of a summer dress against bare legs, the breeze and the still, warm evening sun.

The education part of the week consisted of a few lectures and a full day spent touring CWS factories in Manchester. Other than that, we were free to go to the town, the beach, the pool and the park. After supper, in the evening, there were games and sing-songs and attempts at country dancing. How can I express the feeling of the moment when, for the first time, someone that you've singled out has also singled you out and asks if he can be your partner on the walk or in the dance? We walked, hand in hand, in Hesketh Park in a dream. This was young love, newly minted for us. Never before experienced by anyone. Only we two.

The days went by like pearls counted on a strand.

The venue for this week was a small private girls' school vacated for the holidays. All around us was evidence of their prior claim to the building: bath lists, dorm lists, team lists, notices about the library, and so on. Perhaps this boarding-school atmosphere gave us the idea. On the last day, we decided to have a midnight feast, that very evening. At this point in the week funds were low, but we managed 6d. each and used it to buy lemonade powder to be made up in tooth glasses, sausage rolls, crisps, chocolate snowballs, fancy cakes with lurid icing and swiss rolls. This fare was to be put out in our room and the rest of the girls and the boys were to tiptoe from their rooms when they thought the coast was clear.

We said 'good night' in the normal way as we all trooped upstairs to go to our rooms. Later, when whoever was on duty came round to see that we were all safely tucked up and the lights out, we overacted being asleep or being awakened from sleep, and after she'd gone we leapt out of bed, shone our flashlights and, with suppressed giggles, set out the feast. The girls joined us and then the boys. Those who had dressing-gowns wore them; those who had not, wore their school macs. With many giggles, whispers and nudges we finally sat round in a squashed circle. The adventure had been in actually getting there. What we were supposed to do next we didn't know. It was very tame indeed, just guzzling food. Then someone threw a chocolate snowball at someone else and everyone prepared to throw something when the door burst open and the light was switched on.

We turned towards the door and stayed like that, motionless, as though turned to stone. The person in over-all charge stood there.

'I am pained,' she said quietly, 'shocked beyond belief that you should have broken the rules in this fashion. What will your parents think? What will the Society that sent you here think? You have betrayed the trust placed in you. Go back to your rooms.'

Chastened, crestfallen, humbled, contrite, we slunk shame-facedly out. In the crisis, some that belonged to our room went out and had to come back. It was unnerving. At last we were all in bed and she put out the light. From what she'd said we understood that our parents and our Societies were to be told of our misdeeds. Possibly, we would be forbidden to attend summer school again. We might even be forbidden to attend store classes again. That I might not be allowed to take up my scholarship the following year was of minimal significance when I thought of my crime being reported to my parents and the education secretary. Tears flowed from all of us when we thought of what was about to happen. When there was any chance of the torrents' abating, one or other would repeat the awful words, 'You have betrayed the trust placed in you,' and we were off again.

We were up and about early next morning. The food still lay on the floor where we'd set it out.

In true Angela Brazil tradition, I said, 'I'm going straight to the office to confess. I'm going to tell them it was my idea and that I alone should suffer. Let them punish me if they must, but you should go free.'

Unfortunately, no one else was hooked on Angela Brazil. They didn't say, 'No. We're all in this together. We'll all go,' as I'd expected. They just said it was a good idea and pushed me towards the office.

Of course, when I got inside, I didn't make any noble speeches, I was too intent on saving my own skin and burst into tears as soon as the door closed behind me.

'Does last night mean,' I sobbed, 'I can't come back next year?'

'No. Of course it doesn't,' assured the speaker of the previous evening's stern words. I brightened up – nearly.

'And what about telling my mother and father?'

'We're not going to tell anyone,' she said.

'Does that go for the others, too?' I asked, belatedly remembering those for whom I was going to offer myself up as sacrifice.

'For everyone,' she said. 'The incident is closed. Finished. We hope you'll all be back next year.'

We girls ate up the feast and then went on to eat a hearty breakfast before we left for home. If I was sick on the journey, some merciful angel had expunged it from my memory.

I went back the following year with a different girl – my best friend, in fact. I was a little more restrained as became an old hand at summer schools and it was my friend's turn to go round looking moonstruck. I bragged about the previous year's midnight feast, omitting to chronicle its dismal end. So we had another, only this one was more daring. The boys were to come in through the window. I think this entailed something really intrepid like dropping on to a sort of verandah, running along and being hauled up through the window. This time the food took second place.

As these heroes were heaved into the room there was a bit of indiscriminate kissing in the darkness. The last one had just been hauled into our midst when the door burst open and the light was switched on . . .

After the Junior Stage at store classes was the Intermediate Stage when we studied the lives and times of great men and women. I did a great many other subjects. My pile of certificates mounted and I got the Intermediate Scholarship and set my sights on Holyoake House, the Co-operative college in Manchester.

14. Grammar School v. Job

I loved every day I spent at Bedlington Secondary School. Discipline (at least for girls) was much more lax than it had been at my previous school, the school itself was larger and the classrooms less crowded. Most of all, the ill-health which had bedevilled my childhood disappeared. I got into as much mischief as I could, broke as many rules as I could, thought up as many dodges for getting out of working and doing homework as I could and, in all but the lessons I really enjoyed, I slipped gradually further and further down the form lists.

When I was 13 I suddenly began to think about the future. Until that time, it seemed that these happy days would never end. But, by the time I was 13, gaps began to appear in our numbers. The class began to shrink as one member after another reached his or her fourteenth birthday, the age at which it was possible to start work. Not everyone left at this age, of course, but sufficient did for it to be noticeable.

At that time, a generally held practice for girls was that they started official courting at about 17 or 18, got engaged, saved for

LMcCT
5/85

a bottom drawer and married at 21 or just before. The jobs or careers open to them were limited.

On leaving school at 14, girls could 'go to place', which meant they could go into good service at one or other of the great houses – or even houses of lesser greatness. But, in the years immediately prior to the Second World War, fewer girls in Ashington were taking up this form of employment. Some went to 'help out' in larger houses in the area. Often they went 'half days', that is, they started at 8am or even earlier and left in the early afternoon when they might well have crowded a full day's work into five or six hours and left everything in readiness for the evening meal; the evening dirty crockery and table linen would be washed up next morning. As they were 'only working half a day' there was no need to give them time off, so they were on duty seven days a week and were paid accordingly – perhaps as little as 3s. 6d. (17½p) or 5s. (25p) a week.

A fair number of girls did not go out to work. Instead, they were kept at home. I remember one father saying of his daughter who left the secondary school at 14 because he wasn't going to have her worry herself into an early grave with all that 'book stuff'. 'With three men working, it's a pity if we can't keep one lass at home without her having to work.'

This being kept at home was often a euphemism for being the family drudge. Men and boys working were run after, hand and foot. In return for this, girls had their clothes bought and were sometimes, but not always, given pocket money. One such person to whom this happened was my aunt. I did not, of course, think it strange at the time, but, years after, when she was widowed at the age of 49, I invited her to stay with us for the fortnight. She arrived looking very smart and carrying one small suitcase. As the days passed I was surprised at the number of dresses she'd brought with her, considering the suitcase she'd carried.

'Well,' she said. 'When I made these dresses I had packing them into a small space in mind.'

'You made them yourself?'

'Yes.'

'They're beautiful. I didn't know you'd taken sewing and dress-making lessons.'

'I never have. I always wanted to, but never could.'

'What sort of patterns do you use?'

'None. I design and make every one myself. I made the coat I wore here, too.'

I was aghast. 'You have a fortune in those hands and in that brain,' I said. 'Why on earth didn't you train as a dress-maker?'

'I'd have loved to. There was nothing I wanted to do more. I loved dress-making. But, you see, I had no choice. With six workers I was needed at home.'

I thought it wasn't too late to redress the balance, but she did.

Some years later when I spoke to one of my uncles about it he said, 'Yes. I realize now what a shame it was. When we were going to dances, she laid out clean shirts, collars, gloves and shoes for each of us. And, of course, socks and suits. And, do you know, she never got pocket money? She had a lad so she didn't need any. If they went for a day to the town, she would be given 2s. but it wasn't to spend. It was in case they got separated and she had to pay her own train fare back.'

And she was part of a family who loved her. Her father and brothers did not see anything out of the ordinary in what she did because it wasn't unusual; it was expected.

Shops provided the greatest opportunities for those who wanted a job, from the biggest shops on Station Road to the lesser ones and those that flourished in the back streets. Among the shops, the store stood supreme. Staff here were thought to be paid higher wages than anyone else and, certainly, they worked fewer hours. One young lady employed in the store helped out as an interim measure at a Brownie Pack. On her first evening one of the Brownies asked her if she was a teacher. Before she could reply another said, 'No, she isn't. She works in the store and me mammie says if you can get a job in the store, you're made for life.'

This opinion was fairly widely held at that time and any young lady still working after she had comfortably passed her twenty-first birthday was frequently said to be 'in with the fixtures'. With her good wage she had thought twice about getting married, because, at that time, married women did not work outside the home.

When there were vacancies in the store, notices appeared in the windows of all the Society's branches. Those wishing to apply had to be 14, but not yet 16. Applicants were invited to attend the Arcade Hall on a Monday evening. This was the evening the board of governors, or the committee, met. A test was set. Papers were marked in the order in which applicants finished. Naturally, those whose papers were completely correct took precedence over those with one answer wrong. Usually, up to five were kept back. This was a precautionary measure taken in case the amount spent in the store by numbers one, two, three and four was not up to scratch. It rarely happened that anyone was turned down for that reason. The rules were too well known for that.

Some shopkeepers, when they were interviewing a girl as a possible employee, would ask her if she intended applying for a job in the store should one be advertised. If she said yes, then she didn't get the job she was after. Most said no, and then applied anyway, running the risk of not being selected but still being reported to her boss by a witness which was likely to result in her losing the job she did have. Jobs were at a premium.

There were also office jobs to be had, but, usually, even for the most menial clerical post, a high standard of shorthand and typing was required. In addition, it helped if there was someone willing to put in a quiet word for you.

For all of these situations mentioned above, candidates had to be under 16. Thus, those attending secondary school who did not wish to go on to the sixth form had to leave before they could take School Certificate.

Those who did stay on to the sixth took Advanced School Certificate at about 18 years of age. Then, there were virtually only two courses open to girls: nursing or teaching. The latter required a further two, three or even, four years' training at college or university. This would rule out any thought of marriage for some years to come, for there was an unwritten law that you paid your parents back for the sacrifices they had made on your behalf.

It never occurred to me that I would leave school before I had gone systematically through all forms. Generally speaking, higher education was still frowned upon for girls and considered a waste of time. 'Dress a girl and educate a boy' was a commonly held maxim. Fortunately for me, it was not one to which my parents subscribed. They believed an education would be as valuable to me as it would to my brother and, for this, I am more grateful than I can say, especially as I knew pressure had been put on them not to send me to secondary school. My grandfather took his duties as head of the house very seriously and when my grandmother informed him on his return from the pit that I had called with the news that I was going to Bedlington, he quickly ate, bathed, changed and came down to our house. My grandmother came with him, it was such an important occasion.

I was upstairs tidying my room when they came in. After a while, I heard raised voices and with some trepidation, went quietly downstairs to listen at the door.

'I should have been told before things got this far,' my grandfather was saying. 'You'll rue every hair of your head, sending her there. She'll get above herself and above you. Her job is here, at home, till she's old enough to get a decent lad and get married. Think on. You've got a lad. It's his schooling you should be thinking about. If you've any money to spend on books and things, it should go to him. He's the one you should be thinking of. What good will it do her? Putting ideas into her head. We don't want any girls being made miserable by being educated above their station in this family.'

'Your father is right. Don't sit there shaking your head,' my grandmother put in. 'How long do you think it will be before she can pay you back? And how old will she be then? It's one thing letting her go. It's another thing keeping her there. Have you seen some of them lasses that have gone? Right clips they look when they've grown out of their uniform and can't get another because it costs too much. Them that teach will have to teach all their days. There's nobody good enough for them, or they can't afford to leave their jobs. Besides, she'll never stand up to it. Think of the trouble you've had to rear her this far.'

My grandfather didn't particularly like the limelight taken away from him, especially when he was laying down the law, which was fairly often.

'That'll do, Lizzie,' he said. 'I'm still head of this family. I hope I'm not too old yet, to have me say. And mean it. I'm boss in my house. And,' he went on, apparently addressing my father, 'I expect you to be boss in yours' – obviously, he suspected my mother's hand in this – 'Put your foot down now, before it's too late.'

I stood against the wall next to the door, trembling. I didn't like family rows and I had started this one. I hadn't told my parents that I'd called in at my grandmother's and given them this advance news. Also, I stood in awe of my grandfather and rarely had the courage to speak on my own initiative when I was in his company. His word was law. Perhaps my joy concerning Bedlington would be short-lived.

'It's not a case of that, Father,' my own father answered. 'Peggy Dixon thinks she should go. She sent for us and told us she should make a move. She's nearly been through the school. She's going to spend a long time kicking her heels in Standard Seven if we let her stay where she is. She has a right to her chance. We've made up our minds.'

'It's not up to Peggy Dixon –' my grandfather started, but I waited to hear no more and crept back upstairs. Whatever the outcome of the scholarship, I was to go to Bedlington Secondary or Morpeth High School. I had no idea my mother and father had been up to school. My tidying-up had been half-hearted to say the least. I now set to work with vigour.

At 13 I suddenly realized that I was paying my parents back badly and decided it was time I pulled my socks up and worked to make up for lost time. This sort of mature reasoning, however, does not come in isolation and I began to wonder where I was going. I had no vocation whatever for nursing and I most definitely did not want to teach. Neither did I want to leave school or miss out on Romance. I knew all about Romance. A friend was regularly given a copy of *The Red Letter* and these she passed on to me. Such literature was forbidden in our house so I kept my contraband under the stair carpet on the second stair down from the top. I read these tempestuous love stories at night under the bedclothes with the aid of a torch. This became increasingly difficult when the battery reached the sear and yellow and could not be replaced because the cost to me was prohibitive. When the battery finally expired I had only my grandmother's *News of the World* which, now that I was growing more critical, was not nearly so romantic.

Thus, I was in a dilemma. I longed to earn the right to wear a cap and gown, but I did not want to teach. I did not want to miss out on Love, but I did not want the domestic treadmill that seemed to go with marriage. Altogether, my problems would be solved if I conveniently died at 21. However, when I reflected on the waste of money, not to mention the sacrifice, involved in sending me to college, I thoughtfully lowered the age to 18.

Peggy Tilley was a friend of mine. She never became a best friend but I do not remember us ever quarrelling. We had rather grown apart at school because she had worked all the time and given of her best in all lessons, unlike me. We had gone through school life, so far, more or less together: I had no doubt that we would end up in the sixth form together; especially as I was now bending every effort to see that, in general, my marks matched hers. I didn't know about myself, but I had no doubt that she, at least, would go on to university. We had both passed that emotive milestone, our fourteenth birthdays, when, one Monday morning, she arrived at school in great distress. She had obviously been crying. I got her into a corner.

'I've got to leave,' she said. 'My father says I've got to apply for the job in the store tonight. He thinks it will be far better for mc if I get a job now and start work. He says I might be a bit upset at first but I'll enjoy working and the money I'll get. He thinks I'll be married by the time I'm 21.'

I was almost as shocked as she was by this sudden volte-face and I did not doubt that she would get the job she sought. She was as good as left.

It didn't occur to her to tell me which department of the store was advertising the vacancy, and I certainly did not think of asking. You just applied for 'a job in the store'. The actual department was of little importance; it was getting the job that mattered. No girl would dream of applying for, say, drapery jobs only. If a job in the dairy, starting at 5am, was the one you happened to get, that was the one you took.

'Then this might be your last day at school,' I said.

'Yes,' she answered, and the tears started afresh.

She didn't come back. I worked even harder to improve my over-all position – suddenly realizing how much I loved the lessons, all lessons – but I could not get rid of the feeling that the writing was on the wall for me, too. At no time had my parents ever suggested I should leave, but I knew within myself that I was going to.

A month or six weeks later Peggy appeared at school on a

Wednesday afternoon. She was transformed. I got her to myself and we walked along the path underneath the lab windows.

'What's it really like, being left and working?' I asked.

'It's marvellous,' she replied. 'And I mean that. School was fine and I loved it, but it cost too much. I didn't realize that. You don't when you're part of it. But now I bring money in. You've no idea what it's like. You feel somebody and you *are* somebody and they treat you like somebody. You're actually doing something towards the house. There's a bit more money and things are easier and you've helped to make them easier. It's not just the money you bring in, it's the money you don't take out. The atmosphere at home is different, too. It's unbelievable. I can't tell you how wonderful it is to have money of your own to spend and buy things with. I get a shilling a week. The first week I couldn't bear to spend it, I just kept looking at it. There's a job advertised now. You should think of applying.'

I did. That afternoon I thought of little else. I understood what she meant, especially about money. Many of us – perhaps I should say most of us – didn't get pocket money; we only got what was necessary for school.

I saw the notice in the store window as I walked home. I'd seen these things before in passing, but they'd been of no real interest to me. This time I stopped. Yes. There it was. 'Wanted. A girl 14–16 years. Apply . . .' It was for a grocery department, but I didn't bother with that bit.

Monday was still days away. I had time to change my mind.

On the Monday, even the geometry and literature lessons, both of which I loved, washed over me because of my preoccupation. I looked out of the classroom window to the lawn and the flower-beds, to the caretaker's house and the railway lines. This might be my very last day at school. I might never have another geometry lesson, might never sit at this desk again. I pulled myself up with a jerk. I hadn't even taken the test yet. Even if I did go, there was no guarantee that I'd get the job. In any case, no one was making me go. No one even knew what I was thinking. I could just carry on as if I'd never had the idea in the first place.

As it turned out, it was easy to slip away from the house after tea was over and the washing-up done.

'I'm just going to pop along and see your Aunt Bella,' my mother said.

'I have to go out, too,' I replied. 'I've forgotten a book. I'll have to borrow.'

My father was at work, and my brother out. I took off my school tie, put on my Sunday coat and went without a hat. I hoped my black stockings and black lace-up shoes were not too much of a give away.

As I approached the Arcade it seemed that the entire female population of Ashington between the ages of 14 and 16 were there: tall girls, short girls, fat girls, thin girls, girls who shrieked out their recognition of this one and that one, girls who stood quietly by themselves, girls who stood silently in groups, girls who rubbed their sweating palms and licked lips dry with anxiety – this was their last chance; their sixteenth birthday was perilously near and Mecca was disappearing before their eyes. I slipped into a convenient doorway. It still wasn't too late. Suddenly, there was a movement. The doors had been opened. I joined the slow-moving crowd. Someone tapped my shoulder. It was one of my school fellows, Betty Watts. We nodded to each other without speaking.

As I climbed the stairs, I suddenly decided I wanted this job. Doubt had gone from my mind. I was going to leave school. Having made the decision, I didn't want to hang on in limbo, in school but not of it, till I finally made the grade and got a job in the store.

As the crowd jostled to get through the door at the top of the stairs, Betty and I were separated. At the door, I allowed others to get ahead of me as I took the scene in – the long rows of trestle tables and chairs being systematically filled. Instinct told me to be as near the top as possible and I fiddled with my shoe and took my place in the queue, getting a seat at the top of the third table. In front of me was a plain sheet of paper and a pencil. I put my hand over my eyes for a few moments and offered up a little prayer that my decision was the right one and that I would be able to do well.

When the last girl was in, the two men who had been conducting operations went to the top of the room. One sat down and the other picked up a sheet of paper and remained standing. These were the two committeemen whose particular province was the grocery department. All eyes were turned to the man standing. No one stirred. No one moved. The proverbial pin could have been heard.

'Now GEE-ALLS,' the man standing intoned in an impressive voice. He considered himself to be a 'polite' speaker which meant he made heavy work of his consonants and lengthened his vowels even more than was normal. On this occasion, he spoke in capital letters and exclamation marks. 'SILERNCE if you PLEEASE. When I give the WORRD! you will TORRN THOASE PAYEPAORS OAVOR! and begin! Any gee-all FOWUND TORRKIN! ORR CHEETIN will have HORR PAYEPAORS CANSLED! When you have FINISHED! bring YORR PAYEPAORS OWT HEOR to WERN OF US! THE FORRST GEE-ALL with ORL HOR SUMS RIGHT! Will be FORRST. EFTOR THAT it will be IN ORRDOR OF MARRIT! We will take the FORRST FIVE. THEN – IF THE FORRST GEE-ALL'S MAM'S PORCHAYSES IS RIGHT! – SHE WILL GET THE JERB! If not the next AND SO ERN. DO YOO UNDORSTAAND!' This last was a statement, not a question. RIGHT! BEGIN!'

And if hor mam's porchayses is right . . .

There was a rustling of papers. I turned mine over and found I had to work a set of mechanical arithmetic and problems. They were not very difficult, but the numbers were unwieldy and it would have been very easy to make a slip; moreover, I was prone to careless mistakes. When I had finished there was no sound other than that of brains working, so I started carefully to check my answers. A chair moved. Like a shot, I picked up my paper and presented it to the nearest man. He had marked the first sum when my friend Betty came up. We both had all-correct answers, but I had the coveted first place. When three more girls presented themselves, the rest were told to put their pencils down and go. They filed out quietly.

As one girl passed us, she put out her tongue and said, 'Secondary school snobs. You shouldn't be allowed to try.'

One man collected the papers and pencils while the other disappeared through a door. He had gone to check our parent's purchases. We waited. No one spoke. Presently, the man came back.

'You two stay,' he said to Betty and me. 'The remainder can go.' The three girls left and the man disappeared again.

'There must be two jobs,' said Betty.

The papers and pencils having been collected, we were asked to follow the two men. We were taken to a large, heavy door with 'Boardroom' labelled on it in gilt. I was called in first. It was a large room, down the centre of which there was a huge table with people sitting round it. With one accord they looked at me. The man at the top, Mr Reilly the secretary, told me that as I had met with the conditions laid down – namely, I had completed the test paper accurately and had parents who prudently spent a high proportion of what income they had in the various departments of the AICS – the job in the Hirst grocery department was mine. I was to present myself there, to the grocery manager and buyer, on the Thursday morning following, at nine o'clock. I was to take with me a coat overall. Had I any questions? Any questions! It was with the greatest difficulty I got my dry mouth to say, 'No, Sir. Thank you, Sir.'

I waited for Betty. It turned out there was a temporary post in another department. It was offered to her with the guarantee that the next permanent job that cropped up would be hers.

News of my changed status pleased all my family. I returned my books to school the following morning and went to see the headmaster and his deputy. In the afternoon, my uniform was consigned to the ragbag (not before time) to be turned into clippings for the next mat, my Sunday clothes were demoted and I accompanied my mother to the store's bespoke department to be measured for a suit.

On the Thursday morning I presented myself at the Hirst Grocery, my new overall under my arm. It was my first ever visit to this shop. I wore my erstwhile Sunday coat and an old-fashioned beret as neither my school hat nor my Sunday hat were considered suitable and we (my mother and I) felt I should wear a hat on my first morning. And a very quaint creature I must have looked as I made my uncertain way through the grocery doors. Had I been directed to any other department (notably, the drapery) the girls would have taken me in hand and made me presentable in no time at all. I would have been told immediately that hats were out and that my overall needed shortening and taking in.

But a very different reception awaited me in the department to which I had been sent. I was received with a great deal less than enthusiasm and directed to the Boss's office, a wooden-telephone-kiosk-like erection on a raised platform, as became his elevated position. He had been looking out of the window when I arrived but had retreated into his sanctum before I got to him. I had to knock on the door and wait till I was bidden enter.

I must have been about five-feet one inch at the time, and my weight, fully clothed about seven stone. Still, there was hardly room for both of us in the office which was the width of the roll-top desk that occupied the greater part of what space there was.

'I've – er – I've come about the job,' I stammered.

Mr Joe Dunn looked me up and down as if it was the first he'd heard that he was about to have a new assistant.

'What's your name?' he asked. I told him.

'Your first name?' he persisted. At that time the name 'Linda' was most uncommon. To date, I'd never met another.

'Linda.'

'Lydia.'

'No. Linda.'

'There's no such name. You mean Lena.'(He pronounced it Lee-nor.)

I gave up.

'Well, Miss,' he said, 'the foreman'll show you where to put your coat in a minute. I expect you to work hard. You'll start on the counter. There's a rule in this shop and mind you keep to it. Eat what you like, but take nothing out. Now remember.'

'Yes, Sir,' I whispered with the utmost deference.

He looked at me with a new interest. No one had called him 'Sir' in living memory.

'All right, hinny.' He got up and reached over and opened the door. My staff training was over.

15. Store Lass

Mr Jack Coxon, the foreman, was summoned by a 'how' and a jerk of the head. I followed him in to the office behind the counter in one corner of the shop. Its situation was actually under the stairs that ran between the grocery and greengrocery departments. It was possible for the tallest man to stand upright at one end of this man-made cave, but the other end tapered off to nothing. I didn't realize it at the time, but, cloakroom-wise, this had been the foreman's domain. He hung his outdoor clothes here to distinguish him from the commonalty who hung their coats and jackets in the back shop on the brick wall adjacent to where we kept the soap, candles and washing soda and where, had I been an apprentice, I'd have had to hang mine.

The stairs which allowed for this office accommodation were the rather narrow Victorian type. It follows, then, that the room was not wide. Its door was almost always kept open. In its infancy it had been possessed of four clear panes of glass. Three of these panes now held about half a century's accumulation of dust and dirt while the fourth pane was missing, probably removed by a deliberate hand some years previously. A large piece of cardboard suspended by frayed string from a nail covered the top half of the door. The side of the cardboard seen by those in the office when the door was closed depicted a huge tea-pot, into which a disembodied hand was pouring tea-leaves. The caption read: 'Co-operative Tea Is Filling the Nation's Tea-pot.'

Along the wall, on the hinged side of the door, was the shop's stock of cigarettes ready for sale. The big, unopened boxes were stored in the back shop. Immediately in front of the door was a large Victorian desk, bigger but similar in style to the one Bob Cratchitt worked on in Scrooge's office. It was filled with musty books and ledgers and the current wages book, the book in which the foreman calculated what was due to us minions every fortnight. Above the desk, on the wooden wall, was a picture, dusty and faint with age. It showed a photograph of the employees who had worked in the shop shortly after it was built. Above this was a clock, the instrument by which the staff were meant to take the time for closing. As overactive apprentices had been known to push the minute hand on to hasten that hour, both the foreman and the Boss checked the time against their own watches, before giving the go-ahead for our mass exodus.

On the opposite wall, the one containing the door, there was a bench which ended in a short partition. It was lower than the desk and started before the desk left off so there was little more than just enough room for one person to pass through the gap between the bench and the front of the desk. The wall above the bench, like the upper half of the door, was made up of panes of glass, of which one had been removed, again possibly by design. On the shop side of this wall were shelves on which stood a large variety of seven-pound tins of loose biscuits, almost completely covering the glass. The office side of the wall was spotted with bits of paper curling and yellow with age. They had been nailed or thumb-tacked there for some particular reason long forgotten, by a hand long gone. They were now part of the dusty fixtures. The architect who designed this room had, no doubt, placed the windows in these strategic positions so that they would let in as

The Boss

much light as possible. In this respect, the intention was
thwarted. Nevertheless, the windows were cunningly used, as I
was to find out.

Where the desk ended there was quite a large area of about
one-yard square where there was nothing but floor. In the wall
of this area was the heavy black safe. Then two sizeable black
pipes ran across the width of the room, one above the other to
mark the end of this clear floor space. These were the hotwater

pipes connecting the grocery with the greengrocery for heating purposes. I had to step over these to get to the hook placed on a board tacked to the ceiling for the accommodation of my coat. Beyond that lay a rapidly downward sloping ceiling, about 50 years' rubbish and darkness. A haven for mice. Not even the shop cats at their hungriest went there. A light on a pulley lit the bench area, a static one the desk area.

The foreman pointed to the place where I had to hang my coat and disappeared. I changed into my overall. It wasn't an improvement. This garment was too big and too long. It completely shrouded any potential attractions I might have had.

The shop seemed to go on for ever and all the shelves were packed with goods of all sorts. More and more men seemed to be coming in from the backshop, some still tying their aprons or putting on their white coats. Everyone seemed to have a purpose. Under the watchful eye of the Boss they started work straightaway.

I walked timidly into the shop and hesitated behind the counter. One man was serving and another was filling a fixture. I might as well have been invisible.

'Darseh' – a word that defies translation – said the customer being served. 'Have you started taking in lasses?'

Mr Greener, the tall man who was serving her, folded himself up – no, not 'folded'. That suggests he did something consciously. Rather, chameleon like, he changed imperceptibly, so that he fitted comfortably on to the counter, leaning with his elbow and resting one foot on a fixture below. I felt them both staring at me and I fixed my eyes on to a spot beyond the far wall.

'Yes,' answered Mr Greener. 'It's a great mistake. It won't work. Grocering is a man's job. It's a skilled job. Takes years of training. No girl, or woman either for that matter, is up to it. However, they'll learn their mistake in time.'

Another customer came in. I could do something instead of just standing there.

'Yes?' I said before she got up to the counter.

'You're in a hurry,' she said. 'That's a change. D'you work here now? Ah, well, they'll soon knock that out of you. A quarter of butter.'

I looked round in bewilderment. There was a sudden burst of activity at the door. A smartly dressed woman rushed in and darted round into a little glass kiosk arrangement in the shop area next to the door. In one movement, she took off her things, put them away, picked up a pen, opened a book and began writing. Still bewildered, I looked back to the woman.

'In the back-shop,' she said. 'Through there,' and she jerked her head towards an opening a little to my right. I walked to the place she'd indicated. I looked around. It was huge. There were parcels everywhere, a counter and men working. Then I saw them. Barrels containing quantities of butter. I looked at them but none seemed small enough to be a quarter of a pound.

'What d'you want, hinny?' It was the Boss standing behind me.

'A quarter of butter.'

'There,' and he pointed to a small amount of butter done up in grease-proof paper on a marble slab. He told me the price and directed the young man filling a fixture, George Wade, to show me how to make out a check.

Each member had a check book containing 210 checks. Whenever a purchase was made, the book was proffered and the check written out with the date, the initials of the person serving, the department and the amount. The top copy of the check was torn out and the customer kept the carbon copy in the book in order to ascertain that the right dividend was given. In our shop, the top check went into a wooden box kept on the ledge behind the particular till to which it referred. At the end of the day, the checks were put into an envelope and sent up to the check office, where they were added and compared against the total for the day in the till concerned. Shortages had to be paid for. When a customer forgot to bring the check book, he or she was given a yellow check from the book on the counter. The appropriate check number was written on this yellow slip, but if the person wished to have it credited – i.e. to get dividend from it – the check had to be transferred to the check book. Some people saved these yellow slips up till they had quite a number. Then, just before the half-year ended, they would bring them in to be transferred. This was a most unpopular job, particularly as the yellow checks had to be pinned to the check book check. Not only had the assistant to look for a pin, but there was also the risk of getting 'progged' (pricked) while ramming the day's checks into an envelope.

By the greatest good fortune, the second customer I served also wanted a quarter of butter. Thinking the one I'd got from the slab was a stray, I looked around for the container which held the quarters. Again the question. Again the Boss. I told him what I was looking for. He was incredulous.

'I've just showed you. You'll have to learn quicker than that. You're not going to be much use here if you can't remember for two minutes where the quarters of butter stay.'

Chastened, I picked up the commodity and went back into the shop. There was a lightening of the air. Obviously, the misgivings about the ability of females to work in a real grocer's shop was justified. I flushed in my discomfort.

One of the men came up to me as I stood at a till, waiting for change. He smiled rather absent-mindedly. He had close-cropped, light gingery hair and was so clean he looked as though he'd just been scrubbed inside and out.

'If you want to know anything,' he said, 'ask me. Don't go to anyone else.'

This was Jack McKenzie. I appreciated his kindness and generosity and took full advantage of his offer.

About half-past ten, the Boss again summoned the foreman on my behalf.

'Putteron books,' he said. He looked around and directed his speech at an elderly gentleman putting up a bath of rice in the far corner.

'You'd better extend, Alf, till she gets the hang of it,' he said.

The elderly gentleman, who had the misleading look of a genial Mr Pickwick and an indulgent barbered Santa Claus rolled into one, dug his scoop into the rice and rubbed his hands on his apron. His rosy cheeks became rosier and the gold rims of his glasses glinted determinedly as he moved away from where he'd been working.

The foreman, in the meantime, was making his way along the shop to the little office, a long book under his arm. He gave no indication that I was in any way involved, in spite of the Boss's words. Alf, or Mr Routh as he was more respectfully called, followed him.

When the foreman re-emerged from the office he paused for a moment and said, in the voice of authority, 'Send her in when he's finished extending Weekly Two.' As this wasn't directed at anyone in particular, no one answered. The counter was getting busy and I was getting a little better at serving, especially as George Wade picked out the 'easy' customers and told me to serve those.

In the middle of my serving one customer, he suddenly said, 'I'll finish her off. You're wanted in there,' and he jerked his head in the direction of the little office.

One or two more books had been brought into the office by this time and these lay on the big, sloping desk. On the bench lay the first book mentioned. At the side of the desk, where it sloped, Mr Routh was standing adding up figures in yet another book.

I stood for a moment, ignored.

'What do I have to do?' I asked at last.

'The foreman should have told you,' my colleague muttered as he added up. I made to go back into the shop. He looked up.

'Total the bills,' he said and with hands that used far too much jerky and unnecessary movement for the task assigned to them, he opened the book on the bench and inserted a small piece of carbon paper between the first two pages, near the bottom.

'There,' he said. 'Total them.'

I sat on the stool really meant for the high desk, and bent to my task. I added up the column and wrote down the answer then began checking.

'You total, I check,' said my companion.

I totalled. I went on totalling. Occasionally, someone came in, closed the door to, and got some cigarettes. I looked up hopefully, once or twice, for recognition. None came. Most often my neighbour got a nod, or a 'Now Alf' or a 'Now then, Mr Routh' or, more rarely, from an apprentice a 'Now, Mr Crowth' – at which he either snorted or affected not to hear. And I went on totalling. It seemed I had done nothing else since the beginning of time, yet I had barely reached the halfway mark. By this time, two further books lay on the bench. I shifted on my seat. I stood up, sat down, stood up again, sat down again, all the while totalling.

After an hour and a quarter, 'I've finished,' I said.

'Leave it here,' my superior commanded, 'and start the next.'

I did so, standing up.

Another man came in. His brown eyes were serious behind his glasses and his dark hair was brushed straight back from his pale forehead. 'How goes it?' he asked the elder man. The latter gave a slight snort (he did this very effectively) and shrugged his shoulders.

As the newcomer passed him he pointed to the book I'd done, and said, 'One-and-a-half hours.'

The newcomer, whose name was Bobby McGinley, shook his head and sucked his teeth. From a pocket he took a penknife and from behind his ear, a pencil. With great skill, he sharpened the pencil to a fine needle-point and, replacing it behind his ear, he took another pencil from the top pocket of his white coat. When this was sharpened to his satisfaction he took a book from the desk and began working on it. From time to time, the two men carried on snatches of conversation, but soon this gave way to much tut-tutting and in-drawn whistles from Mr Routh, who had now begun to check my totals. His pencil worked overtime as, with heavy strokes he altered some of my figures. Now, not only was I totalling another book, I was trying to ascertain how many bills he merely initialled and how many he had to alter. There were very few of the former. The sighs, the in-drawn breaths, the clicking of teeth, the shifting of stance, the looks at the clock became more frequent and soon filled the small room.

'They didn't teach arithmetic at that high school of yours then?' said Mr McGinley.

'It was the secondary school,' I replied.

'Same thing.'

'Oh, yes,' I answered, entirely missing the heavy sarcasm in his voice. 'We did arithmetic as well as algebra, geometry and trigonometry.'

'Ha!' snorted Mr Routh. He finished the book and threw it down.

'I'm going,' he said. 'Finishing time or not, I've had enough.'
And putting his pencil in his top pocket with great deliberation,
he strutted out. This 'early finish' sounded more desperate and
militant than it really was. It was already half-past twelve and
the customers still remaining were being hurried out of the shop
which closed from half-twelve till half-one.

I had a long walk home; it took 20 minutes fast going.
Fortunately, my mother did not ask how I'd got on.

'I didn't think you'd have much time,' she said, 'so I've only
made you a pudding.'

What a relief this was! Midday dinner was not my favourite
meal – but this *was* my favourite pudding.

I spent the rest of the afternoon on those wretched books.
Four hours non-stop. I totalled and totalled and totalled and
added up and totalled and added up and taddled and puddled
and tottled up and toppled and people came in for cigarettes and
Mr Routh snorted and whistled and clicked his teeth louder and
louder and witty young men came in giggling to offer Alf a
hammer – Is this any good, Alf? – and he grew redder and the air
got warmer and hotter and I totallped and puttalled and
topplednupted and uptaddledndaddledntaluupedded . . .

At home, we all sat round the table in the early evening having
a meal. Again, my mother had produced my favourite dishes –
home-made mincemeat pies, peas, chips, apple pies and custard.
This touched me very much.

'How did today go?' my father asked.

'Very well,' I said. 'Very well. I think I'm a sort of clerk.'

'That's good,' he replied. 'That's very good. Stick in and work
hard. That's the thing to do.'

I kept my thoughts of the day at bay till I was in bed; in the
privacy of my own room, the tears flowed silently and copiously.
This was to be my life from now on and I hated it. With all my
heart I hated it. All those awful bills and the way hardly anyone
spoke to me. I had gleaned some scraps from the conversation
that had taken place around me while I had been on the counter
and from the fact that one of the customers was the mother of the
man I'd replaced.

I gathered this man had been dismissed. He was very well

liked by everyone but he had 'milked the till' and those in authority had no other choice. It was something neither the Boss nor the Committee wanted to do, but rules were rules. The committee had then decided to advertise for a girl instead of a boy – to keep costs down, I think. Naturally, there was an outcry about this new turn of events, but ruffled feelings had at least been smoothed by the assurance that no female would be in line for promotion; this was a purely male prerogative. In spite of this concession, most men saw my appointment as a threat to their jobs and livelihoods. I think they were calmed with the guarantee that taking on a female hand was in the nature of an experiment. Presumably, if it didn't succeed, it would be abandoned.

While the mother of the unfortunate young man was in the shop, it seemed to me that every one of the men came up to her to express his sorrow at what had happened to his colleague and his anger at the result. I did not, of course, understand the politics of the situation. I knew only of its effect on one miserable 14 year-old-girl.

16. Of Long Stands, Tartan Paint and Flannel Hammers

On Friday, it was back to the books and a very hectic morning.

The entire area served by Hirst grocery was divided into loads. In the early days of the store, the pit paid their men fortnightly. The week on which they were not paid was called 'Baff Week'. Then, the store order men went out for orders on a fortnightly basis. However, long before I became one of 'the store lasses', the pit-men had been paid on a weekly basis. A few fortnightly loads remained, but these were light, except at Newbiggin. Newbiggin had its own store, but, for some reason, many people who lived there preferred to deal with Ashington store. Thus, there were still two fortnightly loads at Newbiggin which operated on alternate weeks. The Newbiggin order men took the current week's order at the time they took the money for the previous order. Those living in Hirst came to the shop to pay for their fortnightly order. For the rest there were Weeklies One, Two, Three, Four and an embryo Five. The first four loads were the biggest. Each had two books, a large and a small, so making Weekly One, part 1, and Weekly One, part 2, etc. Each large book contained 100 triplicate pages and each small book 50.

As soon as the orders were completed on Thursday and Friday mornings, there was a rush to get the books extended (that is, checked to see that all items had been charged for), totalled, checked and the books written up. This last task was the job of Miss Rose Lynch, the woman who had made such a whirlwind entrance when I was about to serve my first customer. It was always a rush because Friday was pay day at the pit and the order men (who were officially journeymen grocers) liked to get to the houses of certain of their customers to claim their share of the pay before it all went. This particular Friday, it seemed, they were later than usual and the fault was my ineptitude. In time I learned that they were always later than usual.

When the books were finished, I returned to the counter to serve. During the afternoon Miss Lynch had a word with me and asked how I was getting on. I told her things were going fine and she said she was sorry she hadn't spoken to me earlier, but Thursdays and Friday mornings were busy times, as I'd find out.

Once again, I reserved my tears for the privacy of my room.

This nightly weeping lasted about a fortnight, at the end of which time changes were taking place. Looking back, it is easy to see that several things contributed to my unhapppiness during those early days as a store lass.

Naturally, the men would be of one accord when they saw (or thought they saw) their livelihood threatened and their métier as grocers undermined. It was a man's job; it could not be done by a female. Also they knew how to treat apprentices.

These boys came at intervals of a little over one a year. The youngest went the errands or messages. The chatelaines of the local aristocracy who possessed telephones simply rang up whenever they ran out of something or wanted some goods, sometimes only one or two small items. When this happened, the messenger boy stopped whatever he was doing and got on the heavy shop bike with the huge basket in front and delivered the order. He was also at the beck and call of every other person in the shop because everyone was above him. So, often, the only official communication he had with his elders and betters was, 'Fetch this,' 'Get that.' When the Boss required his services – or, indeed, the service of any apprentice – he merely shouted. 'How there.' It was left to the apprentices to judge from the tone of voice who was needed. As they reached the final stages of their

It was the apprentices' job . . .

apprenticeship, the Boss usually modified the command to an 'How – er – um – er,' or even the soon-to-be journeyman's first name.

With a girl there was no established form of behaviour, so they waited. Also, Thursdays and Fridays were busy days. They had no time to wrestle with attitudes towards this stranger in their midst.

For me, I had never yet been in a situation like this. Born into an extended family in an enclosed community, I had never really entered any situation where I didn't know anyone.

I appreciated none of this, of course, in those early days. However, I did understand one thing, or I thought I did. The reason I was not accepted was because I knew nothing and because I could not do the same work as the others. My evenings, so recently full of homework, were now free. I made a rough plan of the shop, back shop and warehouse, and 'placed' the stock – especially that for which there was little demand – and these placings I learned.

The Hirst Grocery stood directly opposite the Society's Arcade premises. The entire shop was huge and consisted of the front shop, the back shop, the cellars and the warehouse. The back premises of all the departments on that side of the road opened on to a cobbled yard, which was called the grocery yard because the grocery was, by far, the largest department. For convenience of unloading flour and grain, a huge, heavy sliding-door operated at the far end of the warehouse. Other than that, goods were delivered at the double doors of the back shop. Here, too, the horse and flat, under the guidance of Billy Marks and his apprentice assistant, was loaded up with the various parcels and boxes to be delivered to customers.

The front shop was large and rectangular in shape. On one long side was the provision counter, the door, Rose Lynch's tiny office, a window and, in the corner, the Boss's office. The short side adjacent was all counter. Next to it was the other long side. Here, in the corner, was an opening into the back shop, with another opening midway down the side. This opening provided access to the back shop direct from the front of the shop to the back. Thus, it cut the long counter in two, the second half of which was the main serving counter. The short side connecting this counter with the provision area was also a counter, the one part of the shop that would be hidden from the Boss as he stood on his steps, his eye on his Empire.

This was mainly because of the pill cabinet, the biscuit display stand and a further random display of stands which made way for the bacon machine. The pill cabinet was a large receptacle with a glass front, a door at the back and a number of glass shelves and compartments. It was full to the brim with numbered yellow boxes whose contents were made at the CWS drugs factory at Droylsden. In their entirety, these concoctions claimed to cure any ailment, any pain or discomfort under the sun. All you had to do was to tell whoever was serving you or taking your order how you 'were held', and then the assistant would look at the appropriate ailment on the sheet and tell you what number pills you should take. The charge was 6d. (2 ½p) a box.

Some people were accredited with more medical knowledge than others. 'D'ye mind if I have a word with Willie?' you'd be asked. 'No offence, pet. He just understands the way, I'm held . . . Willie, I've got this pain. It starts here and it goes round to here.'

'Have you been to the doctor?'

'No. It's not bad enough for that yet. I just thought you might tell me what I can take to get a bit of ease but like.'

'Do you get it all the time?'

'No. To tell the truth, it's just after a washing day when I'm – when I've – well, you understand.'

'Give her some of them 45s. Try them and see how you get on. If they don't do any good, I'd have a word with the doctor.'

'I'll do that, but I must say I don't like bothering him. There's others worse off than me need him more. I knew before I asked you would put me on the right track.'

Hiding behind the pill cabinet was the cheese counter. Most often this contained a huge piece of American cheese, a lesser piece of crumbly Cheshire, a small piece of Gorgonzola and an Edam. All cheeses spent some time down in the far cellar where they were turned regularly till they were judged ready for the counter. The American cheese was rather like a huge cylinder in shape. It was cut into three equal rounds by means of the cheese-wire. This was a piece of strong, thin wire with small metal bars at either end for gripping. The person cutting the cheese put the wire at the back, one knee against the cheese and pulled. For smaller amounts, the cheese knife was used. This was a metal semi-circle with a sharp knife-edge and a handle. Cheshire cheese was cut in a similar way.

The most popular cheese was the American variety, which was used extensively for pit baits (packed meals). The two most popular types of bait were cheese sandwiches or jam sandwiches. When a customer asked for a quarter or a half pound of cheese, that is what she got. Amounts were cut with remarkable accuracy – if anything, perhaps a little overweight. This extra was never charged for. The shelf immediately under the cheese counter contained sheets of paper cut to suitable sizes for wrapping cheese. This cutting of paper was one of the jobs the apprentices did at the bidding of a counter-hand.

The biscuit display stand stood next to the pill cabinet, but on the customer side of the counter. It was not as high as the pill cabinet but high enough to hide behind, if necessary. In it, a number of tins of biscuits were kept on display. No one ever looked at them and they were often forgotten for months on end till the biscuits became pale and wan from neglect, and, in their anaemic state, indistinguishable from one another.

In the fixture underneath this counter area was a long, shallow, oblong box containing whole almonds. A few quarters already weighed and put into 'pokes' (made by twisting a square of grease-proof paper into a cone shape) lay on top of the almonds. In the next fixture was a box of citron peel – large, hard bits of orange, lemon and lime peel with sizeable rock-hard bits of sugar sticking to them. It, too, would have a number of quarters lying already made up. This time the grease-proof paper was folded into a square packet with flaps at either end tucked in. Cherries were also kept in these fixtures and wrapped in a similar way. These commodities were put up by the counter-hands at the end of the counter next to the main counter. They used the slender upright scales with their circular brass pans and delicate needle. Except at Christmas, only small quantities were put up.

For the rest, the dusty recesses of the fixtures in this short counter held cardboard advertisements with missing stands, tins of unpopular stock that had been housed here temporarily and forgotten and a superfluity of leaflets which someone had intended to put to use, but never had.

The provision counter was like all other counters in that it was made of thick, solid wood designed to endure till the Last Trump. However, the top was different. The bacon counter and one next to it were topped with marble. The former had a glass panel at the front to protect cut provisions from direct contact with customers. All other counters had dark-mahogany tops, polished and – here and there – scarred with much use. The bacon counter was marked off by the bacon machine at one end and the cooked meats slicing machine at the other. Sides of bacon and hams were kept hanging from lethal-looking hooks in the far cellar, the coldest part of the shop. We normally only bought in York hams in bulk at Christmas, but the store chemist was partial to this fare and, at intervals throughout the year, we ordered York hams for him specially.

When a new side of ham or bacon was needed, the bacon man or one of the senior apprentices brought it to the front shop and laid it on the marble counter next to the cheese counter, scattering any display that might happen to be there. If the bacon man, Joe Murray, did the scattering, he was allowed to swear at the fool who had put the display on in the first place. If an apprentice did it, he had to put the display back again, naturally without swearing.

In all but the coldest weather, the bacon was washed over with a solution of vinegar and water before it was boned. The boning knife was a long, thin knife honed down to almost stiletto proportions. With a swift, certain movement, Joe would run the knife down either side of the bone and lift the latter out clean, not the slightest fragment of meat sticking to it. In warm weather, the sides and hams had to be scraped clean of maggots first and washed twice or thrice in vinegar and water.

Large tins of cooked meats, those used for cutting up, were

also kept in the cellar.

Underneath the bacon counter were fixtures and shelves mostly containing grease-proof paper and boxes; it was into them that bones were dropped to be sold in pennorths for broth.

The fixtures and drawers underneath the main serving counter were virtually never used for commodities. Instead, they contained balls of string, bags and papers and half a century's accumulation of stuff pushed out of the way to be dealt with later, but forgotten.

The drawers under the next counter contained various kinds of tobacco, rolls of thin, medium and thick twist, long bars of plug, packets of shag, ounces and half-ounces of plug, flake and twist. Loose tobacco was cut off as it was needed, the person doing the cutting using his own pocket knife. There were also clay pipes (rarely sold nowadays), cheroots and cigars and tins of snuff in these drawers. The cigars appeared only at Christmas. I tried taking snuff in the same way as I had tried smoking and, with great daring, going down to the Angler's Arms, Sheepwash, for a drink. Of the three, the only one I really enjoyed and could have continued in, was taking snuff. I found the sensation pleasant – but, of course, it was hardly a practice that I could take up. (Fortunately for me, I abandoned smoking very quickly and drank hardly at all.) These drawers also contained matches, the most popular of which was, with us, Three Torch. This was because we saved the outer wrapping for gifts. As a result of this, the drawer often had a fair quota of loose matches, because if a customer asked for one box, the person serving would open up a packet of twelve, keep the outer cover and deposit the other eleven boxes among the loose ones. This was not always possible, however, because the match drawer was on the list of things that came under the Boss's close scrutiny.

'I've counted them matches in that drawer and there's 114 loose boxes: 114! Now, if that's the only way them among you that's sweetheartin' can give your lass a present, just give her up. Because I want that draw cleared of loose matches before the week is out.'

Empty fixtures had a use when parcels were being put up. To save constant walking to the far ends of the shop and back shop for fish paste and washing soda, a number of such articles were placed in the empty drawers or fixtures and used in the parcels as needed. Unfortunately, those not used were rarely put back. This called for another edict.

'I've just counted the things left in them fixtures. Six tins of peaches, two tins of pink salmon, seven boxes of cheese, eleven tins of peas, a bottle of syrup of figs, three tins of Health Salts and two pound of candles that's been there that long the spiders think it's a hotel. Now, I don't know whose thinking of having a party down there, but, whoever it is, I want that fixture cleared – and see that it stays that way.'

Naturally, the job of clearing fell to an apprentice.

Between the counters and the fixtures proper was an area of floor always thickly covered with sawdust which was changed daily. Before the men left the shop at the front door, they cleaned out the turn-ups of their trousers depositing little mole-hills of sawdust. The sawdust kept the floor pristine and shining.

The walls of the shop were covered in fixtures, as was one wall in the back shop. At the main serving counter, the fixtures were kept full, or 'faced off', with the bright labels from a myriad foodstuffs. These included the extra stock of seven-pound tins of biscuits placed in the fixtures next to the high ceiling, and lower down, the CWS jams and marmalades in pound and two-pound jars – some contained in the older type stone jars and some in the new-fangled glass jars – the tins of Lyle's Golden Syrup and CWS black treacle, and bags of CWS self-raising flour found in the bottom row of fixtures next to the floor. In between were CWS, Crestona and Bero cake mixes, CWS penny bun mixes, CWS tea in brightly coloured packets indicative of their quality, bottles of Camp and Shieldhall coffee, packets of CWS Lutona cocoa, large, medium and small tins of pears, peaches, apricots, pineapple chunks and fruit salad with their CWS names, Adonis, Ajax, Lockreel, tins of milk – evaporated, condensed, skimmed and full-cream – Nutrix, the CWS flaked milk food, CWS jellies, Force, Porridge Oats, cod-liver oil . . . in short, the fixtures were laden with as many goods as possible to attract the customer and remind her of what she needed or might need while she stood waiting for her turn.

Each customer served, each order given and paid for, was a transaction between at least two people, a communication, a relationship between people. There was a fellowship at the counters even when we were at our busiest.

The short side was also full of fixtures from floor to ceiling, also colourful, also on display. It began with the wide selection of Crumpsall biscuits, chief among them those cream crackers so familiar to every member of a men's club, for every weekend they would be eaten with American cheese. Next were the fixtures full of tinned meats, fish, sauces and almost every one of Heinz 57 varieties with their CWS counterparts.

The less colourful, but very necessary, foodstuffs were to be found at the other end of the shop, while the back shop held the stock of candles, soaps and the like.

A ledge ran round the front shop on the fixture side at counter height. Above it were a number of small drawers each having a Latin abbreviation printed on in gilt-and-black lettering. These drawers were rarely used and, one day, I went round opening each one to find out what was inside. Many were empty, rest-homes for spiders living out their lonely but, if size was anything to go by, comfortable existence. In the rest I found a few sticks of thick, rock-hard black liquorice, caraway seeds, cloves, nutmegs, boracic powder, seidlitz powders, senna pods, angelica and curry. This unwanted stock had lain there so long its pungent odour was overpowered by the mustiness of countless years.

On the ledges themselves stood the wooden boxes for checks (one for each till) and, in cardboard boxes, the shop's stock of confectionary, liquorice all-sorts and coconut daisies; large tins held the black bullets and pear drops. We also had a minute quantity of CWS chocolate and a slightly larger quantity of Cadbury's 2d. bars of milk chocolate. At Christmas, the Boss widened his horizons a bit in this field and we sold boxes of chocolates, Chinese figs and Turkish delight.

The butter counter ran the distance between the two back shop entrances. It had a marble slab, in the centre of which was the butter scale, a heavy one with a glass plate on which to place the butter for weighing. A cask of Danish butter would be tipped on to the marble slab to the right of the scale and the butter cut through four or five times with the butter-wire, which was similar to and used in the same way as the cheese-wire. Afterwards, the butter was made up into saleable quantities and put in the empty butter casks placed in line on the floor to the left. New Zealand butter came in square boxes as did lard, except the best quality which came in bladders (pure lard put into pigs' bladders).

A little gangway was left running alongside the butter counter. On the other side of this were opened cases of Silver Seal margarine, Red Seal margarine, Shortex, Silver Medal lard, Sutox shredded suet, boxes of New Zealand butter in quantities, and bladder and ordinary lard in quantities. In the centre space in the back shop was an area kept clear for parcels, the remainder being for goods in bulk. On the wall opposite the butter counter there was a square earthenware sink and a cold tap. Huge unopened boxes of cigarettes were piled against the remaining wall at one end of which, in the corner next to the double doors, a cask of vinegar stood in a little pool of lonely vinegar tears. The décor of the whole was of untreated red brick adorned with spiders' webs and dusty crevices.

The steps leading to the cellars were steep and made of concrete. Going down could be a hazardous undertaking till you could feel your way along the wall to put on the light. When the fixtures were being filled (an ongoing job) and if there was no one about, whoever was doing the filling simply flung the empty carton down the steps. If this went on for any length of time, the clutter at the bottom of the steps became a pile, when, inevitably, it came to the notice of the Boss in his perambulations.

'I've nearly broke me neck on them cellar stairs. I counted 153 cartons down there. For all we know, Billy Marks is buried underneath. Now, I'm going up the yard for a Jimmy and I want them boxes tidied away before I get back.' Naturally, an apprentice cleared them up.

The principal inhabitant of the first cellar was the huge, black, ancient, coke-fired boiler that provided heating for all the store premises our side of the road. Keeping it company was the pile of coke needed to satisfy its voracious appetite. Also in evidence were the long implements used to purge it daily of the excreta clogging its ageing mechanism.

The second and much larger cellar contained, in the centre, barrels of various quantities of butter (Danish) still intact, and other barrels already put up in quantities, boxes of the cheaper New Zealand butter, either intact or put up, and unopened boxes of tinned milk and any other stock that had to be kept in cold conditions. Round the sides were the deep shelves that housed the cheeses. At the very back of the cellar, on a wide shelf, were piles of new order books and, near them, tied in bundles with string, gathering dust, were old order books, dated and in weekly bundles.

Next to the vinegar cask in the back shop was a short flight of wooden stairs that led to the warehouse. To the immediate left of the top of these stairs there was a lift, an elongated box with one side missing. It was operated by a rope and was the same age as the boiler, or, possibly, older. It connected the warehouse with the cellar and creaked and groaned as, with rheumatic jerks, it transported heavy stock to and from the cellar, each trip a triumph of senility over its allotted life-span.

The first and smaller part of the warehouse was given over to unopened sacks of dry goods for the front shop. The fixture which surrounded this area contained quantities of sugar paper and sugar bags in varying sizes and colours. The remainder f the warehouse was almost completely taken up with sacks of flour, both white and wholemeal, chick feed, chick meal, bran, dog biscuits, oats, pigeon corn, Indian corn and every other sort of corn and grain needed to satisfy the appetite and promote the growth of chickens, hens, banties and pigeons. A faint coating of flour covered everything, including the two warehousemen whose domain this was.

At the far end of their territory they had a bench and a number of bins for the flours and grains currently being used. They made these up into the quantities needed for the front shop and packed them into their fixtures. Over the bench was the solitary window-pane, which had been relieved of its coating of dust flour and cobwebs in order that the warehousemen, Billy Benns and Nichol Shears, might look out on to the world beyond.

The warehouse floor was made of wood and was swept daily by an apprentice. The cellar and back shop floors were made of cement and were swept intermittently by an apprentice. The sawdust in the front shop was swept up and replaced from a box every night just before closing time by an apprentice. The rest of the front shop was covered in linoleum which had once been colourful but was now a patchy sludge-grey. It was swept every morning by an apprentice and scrubbed once a week (on hands and knees) by one of the store cleaners.

I soon became aware that Mr Routh was an authority on prices. He had a small black book, alphabetically annotated, and here he kept the price of everything we sold. He could be relied upon to keep his prices up to date. I bought a similar book and filled in the commodities and prices in the evenings from the scrappy notes I'd put in my overall pocket during the day, and I memorized them. I jotted down figures and totalled them endlessly to give me greater skill on the books. I tried doing the work of some of the apprentices, such as sweeping behind the counters and putting down sawdust.

As I became more knowledgeable, and thus more confident, I began to find the hatred I felt for the job disappearing. The more I learned, the more interested I became. These efforts on my part, however, did not guarantee acceptance. Had I known anything about human nature, I would have realized this. The shop did not have the ethos of school, where, if you worked hard and improved, the rewards came not only in examination results, but in the attitudes of the teachers who warmed to you because you were responding to their tuition. The real value of my efforts at this time was personal, a happy side-effect and not the one I aimed for.

There was, however, a gradual thawing-out among some of the staff. No. Here I'm being a little harsh. Some members of staff had never been frozen; they did not need to thaw out. Jack McKenzie had been friendly and more than helpful from the beginning. Rose Lynch was also helpful and willing to talk from our first encounter. What made this more difficult, in her case, was the goldfish bowl situation of her office. Albert Daniels, one of the assistants, asked me, on my first Saturday, where I lived and when I told him he asked what I did for tea on Fridays and Saturdays. (We had half-an-hour's tea-break on these days.) I told him that on Fridays I went to tea at an aunt's who lived nearby, but this was not possible on Saturdays.

'Then,' he said, 'you must come to tea at my house. I live not far away in Woodhorn Road.' And throughout my time at the store I did just that. Every week his wife would have a beautifully set-out, delicious meal of home-made scones, fruit tart and cakes waiting for me. He had a small daughter, Jean, and together we chatted, Jean, Mrs Daniels and I, while the fire burned with a warm, benign flame reflected in our faces. No wonder I was often late back to work.

But perhaps it was the apprentices who did most to break the ice. When I first joined the store, there were five apprentices, I think, with one young man – John Riddell – just out of his time. I had never spoken to this young man, but I knew him. He was extremely good-looking with dark eyes and a wealth of coal-black, wavy hair. He reminded my friend and me of Sir Launcelot in *Morte D'Arthur*, and my friend was passionately in love with him. While this passion lasted (almost a whole month during the winter), on the nights we went to the store classes or were supposed to be at each other's houses, we used to walk past his door, usually four times on each occasion.

As we neared, my friend would grasp my arm and say, 'I can't look. What if he should come out. I'll die if that happens. I just will. Let's turn back.' We didn't, of course, and when we got past she'd say, 'Did you see anything? I had my eyes closed.'

Twice when we passed the door, it opened. The first time, a stream of light made a path in the yard and a tall man – his father, I think – came out holding a paper and wearing a flannel shirt open at the neck and minus a collar. His trousers were concertina'd because his braces had been released from duty. He had probably just come in from the pit, had his meal and his bath and was now going across the road.

As she'd had her eyes shut, I felt I could not tell my friend this less than romantic truth so I said, 'It was him. It was. He stood there in the doorway like a film star. I wish you'd seen him, he looked so handsome.'

'Did he see us?'

'He didn't see me. He only had eyes for you. If you'd seen the way he looked at you!'

'Is he still there? Don't look. Don't. Is he still there? If we went back do you think we'd see him? Don't look. Don't let on we're interested.'

We turned back but the door was shut.

The second time it was his mother, who'd come into the yard to drain a pan of potatoes. I couldn't say it was him because of the smell of potatoes but I said I'd looked through the door and seen him sitting at the table, all handsome. One evening a week he practised in the store hall with the store orchestra. We used to creep up the stairs and try to push the swing-doors open just enough to be able to see him, but not enough for anyone to notice. I also wanted my share of looking – not to see him, I have to confess, but to watch the expression on the faces of the musicians as they toiled and the expression of the conductor who toiled even harder. During this time, I don't think she was ever in his company, nor did she speak to him. In his present exalted position, I didn't feel that I was worthy of his speaking to me.

The senior apprentice was Tommy Bourne, who was almost out of his time. He was an extremely quiet, conscientious and friendly young man. Diffidence had kept him from speaking on the first two days, but after that we became friendly and this friendship persisted throughout my stay.

Thinking to please Mr Routh, who was required to extend books for me, I said to him after the passage of about three weeks. 'I can extend for myself now.'

He brushed my offer aside. 'You don't know the prices,' he said.

'I do, and if I can't remember, I have a book,' and from my pocket I produced my new book, flicking over the pages to let him see the prices were all there. I had to wait many years till I, too, was getting long in the tooth before I understood the folly of what I did that day. He did not answer, but threw the book he was about to extend on to my bench.

It was a mistake in another way. Simply knowing the prices was not enough. I was so unskilled that I had to follow every line to see if any item had been missed and, often, I had to do laborious calculations to see that the correct price had been charged for unusual quantities. It took forever. Later, I knew just by looking at a page whether anything was missing and familiarity made it easy for me to check unusual prices. But that was later. Now, my eyes became glazed and my vision blurred as I toiled and I took longer and longer with each book. Finally, I skipped detailed checking to speed things up. It was an act which was to have future repercussions. The person who totalled was responsible for the extending; the person who checked was responsible only for the total.

The three younger apprentices had not yet acquired the dignity assumed by a near-journeyman. One day, shortly after I made the mistake outlined above, two of them came to me as I toiled alone in the office.

'Do you know what a ball-bearing mousetrap is?' they asked, their eyes alight.

Glad of this interruption and show of friendliness I smiled and said, 'I've no idea.'

'A tom-cat,' they answered and went off doubled up with laughter.

In spite of the *News of the World* and *The Red Letter*, I was incredibly naive at that time. In any case, I'd given up this reading matter when I became a Guide. I was now intent on covering my arm with badges and struggling to live up to the Guide Law:

> Trusty, loyal, helpful,
> Sisterly, courteous, kind,
> Obedient, smiling, truthful,
> Pure as the rustling wind.

On good days I might get as many as five out of ten for effort. It was uphill work, but I never gave in. I hadn't the least idea why the apprentices laughed so much, but I was glad they'd spoken to me and I laughed as much as they.

I'd heard all about Long Stands, tins of Tartan paint and flannel hammers from my uncles. Emboldened by their success with the mousetrap joke, the apprentices sent me to the butchery department for a Long Stand and I waited patiently to be told I'd better try another department and was sent to the cobbler's. I went to the hardware for a tin of Tartan paint and dutifully reported they'd none in stock but were expecting some any day. Flannel hammers, too, were in short supply.

A great deal of friendly goodwill existed between staff and customers, nearly all of whom were regulars. Some customers had a favourite by whom they liked to be served. They never came into the shop unless they knew their particular blue-eyed boy would be there. If the man in question was working in the back shop when one of these customers came in, he would be sent for and usually he cheerfully went to serve, even if he was very busy. Jack McKenzie and Billy Ruddick were both prime favourites in this field. To a lesser degree, so was Jack Greener (the man who'd first acquainted me with the knowledge that women were unfit to be grocers). He was called 'The Raj' among the apprentices because of his way of almost holding court with our more affluent customers. Generally speaking, the men who had weekly loads and Newbiggin loads regarded any of the customers who came into the shop as 'theirs' if they happened to be on their load. There was, indeed, a great deal of personal service.

A few customers were awkward. They were known as 'stumers'. Often they were allocated, unofficially, to one or other of the staff with whom they had struck up a reasonable relationship. For instance, sweets were never weighed, and loose vinegar was never measured. People bought 'two penn'orth of black bullets, hinny; I have a mat in', and were given a generous quantity wrapped up in a poke made of a square of grey paper. Usually, a can was brought for threepenn'orth of vinegar and this can was filled up. As vinegar was threepence a pint and the can held slightly more than a pint, they got good measure.

Occasionally, the Boss put his foot down and ordained that all sweets would be weighed and all vinegar measured. This edict would last a fortnight at most, and would be implemented only when either the Boss or the foreman was actually in the front shop. Most customers recognized this and put up with it, some grudgingly. This was especially true of sweets.

One customer regularly refused to have her vinegar measured in that way. She demanded she got her vinegar can filled as usual. She was one of our well-to-do customers to whom the loss of a small quantity of vinegar was negligible. In the battle of wills, it was the Boss who had to climb down. None of us liked this and our resentment on his behalf was directed towards the customer who had created this situation. She was a 'stumer'.

I had a stumer. Her only fault was that she talked too much about her gifted family who leapt from one pinnacle of success to another. The first time I served her I listened with real interest, adding congratulatory comments of my own. She had come in for a tin of condensed milk, 'the very best'. I said that CWS was every bit as good as Nestlé's but she couldn't agree until I also mentioned it was cheaper – at which point she said she'd try the CWS on my recommendation. When she'd gone, they told me she would have bought CWS anyway without any help from me and also that, in future, she was my stumer.

I was summoned one day from the back shop to serve her. It was a quiet day. The shop was empty save for The Raj and an apprentice eating his way through a pile of corned-beef scraps at the bacon counter. He was 'looking after' the counter till his superior came back. Before we got down to the commodity she'd come in to buy, I heard of the latest family good fortune, news of which had come by letter only that morning. As I listened, I was aware that the youngest apprentice, who had passed me on his way to the cheese counter, was now creeping towards me crouched below counter height. The fourth apprentice was also creeping towards me in similar fashion from the other side.

I said, 'Ah,' involuntarily on an in-drawn breath as I felt my ankles being grabbed. It was the wrong thing to say at this juncture of the episode being related and I pleaded a sudden pain in my side.

By the time she'd got to, 'But you've made me forget what I came in for with all your chatter and questions. A tin of mustard,' my ankles were tied together by scratchy yellow string and the apprentices had crept to the shelter of the pill cabinet, taking the shop scissors with them. The apprentice at the bacon counter had deserted his post and, with a handful of corned beef to sustain him, watched my discomfort with his co-skivers. I tried to break the string by moving one leg quickly and fell against the counter.

'My side,' I said helplessly. 'What . . . what sort of . . . mustard did you want?

'Colman's. *I always buy the best.*'

'CWS is very good,' I countered, wondering how on earth I was going to get away. One of the practical jokers walked from the cheese counter to the back shop smiling in the most friendly way to my stumer and remarking on the weather.

'What a nice young man,' she said. 'No. The CWS might be good, but not good enough.'

'It's cheaper,' I said forgetting, in my extremity, to phrase this in a more acceptable way. She was offended.

'Since when,' she said, 'have I bought anything because it's cheap? I *always* buy the best, as you should know.'

There was no further reason for me to linger, but I stayed

where I was and the mustard stayed where it was – at the other end of the shop.

'Do you *mind* if I have that mustard? Or do I have to go elsewhere?' she said.

'Of course,' I stammered. 'Of course.' At that moment the bacon man returned with a side of bacon on one shoulder and the boning knife in his hand. He bobbed down without dislodging the bacon, flicked the knife upwards and released me.

New, unopened seven-pound tins of biscuits were kept on the very top shelf. A pair of tall steps were kept in the back shop, but they were rarely used. When something from the top fixtures was wanted, one of the younger men obligingly climbed the fixtures, manoeuvred the tin or container to the edge of the fixture, tipped it over and a colleague waiting below skilfully caught it.

Mondays were quiet days. Not being conversant with the innermost workings of the establishment, I did not know that, in the afternoon, the Boss was in the habit of putting his feet on desk, leaning back in his swivel chair and having forty winks. There were glass panes on three sides of his habitat, but they began six feet off the ground. There were counters on three sides of the shop, the first beginning immediately next to the Boss's office. When he wasn't 'on books' Mr Routh usually stood here putting up stock. He had just finished one bath. He announced he was going 'for a pipe' and left. Two of the apprentices brought in the large steps and positioned them sideways to the fixtures. The third apprentice appeared with a sheet of paper and a pencil.

'I have to list these top fixtures,' he said to me. 'D'you mind running up them steps and shouting down what's up there?'

Now, I had no head for heights and I didn't like going up ladders, but I was determined to do what was asked of me so I went up the steps beyond the point where I could hang on to the flat piece at the top. As I made to turn to look at the fixtures, someone shook the steps ever so slightly. Afraid I was going to lose my balance, I put my hands out to the glass panes in front of me with a startled yelp. And, looking down, I saw the no less startled Boss rudely awakened from his nap. I recovered my

Stumer

equilibrium. The Boss recovered his. He got up. As he opened the door the apprentices disappeared.

'What are you doing up there?' The Boss was angry, very angry.

'I'm – er – I'm checking – er – stock in the top fixtures.'

'Come down off there *at once*. And never let me see you up them steps again. When I want that stock checked, I'll ask for it. You might have had a nasty accident.'

I came down the steps red and shame-faced. 'I'm sorry,' I mumbled.

'Sorry!' He swore and made to go back to his office. It was the only time he spoke to me in anger. At the door he turned.

'Get back to the counter,' he said, then added loudly, 'and no more tricks like that.'

After he'd gone, it was a subdued group that returned to their labours and a very angry Mr Routh who had come into the back shop at the tail-end and summed the situation up. He was furious because the Boss had come out of his office and found him, Mr Routh, missing.

Later, the erstwhile heart-throb of my friend pronounced on the incident and made the whole thing worthwhile for me.

'I'll say this for you,' he said. 'You're a good sport.'

17. Committee Men

The Board of Management was always called 'the Committee'. The men who made up the Board were called Committee Men. They were mostly miners or employees of the Society and they met every Monday evening to discuss its business. They also attended Co-op conferences on a rota basis. Usually they worked in pairs, each pair being assigned to one or other of the Society's departments where their duties consisted mainly in weekly visits to the department and in doing the half-yearly stock-taking.

As far as jobs in the Store were concerned, all appointments were made on Monday evenings when the Committee met. Then the (usually) very grateful young persons would meet the Committee *en masse* for the only time in their lives unless they did something which resulted in getting the sack. For those in line, promotions throughout the Society were automatic. No senior posts were advertised for. When Mr Dunn, the General Manager and Buyer of the Grocery Department, retired, all the managers and foremen moved up one. The grocer promoted from the counter to fill the smallest one-man shop on the periphery of the Ashington Store's little empire would be the man who had served the Society longest.

Archie Summers, newly-elected Committee man

Ideally, Committee Men had to be totally committed to the co-operative movement, to its ideals and its workings. They needed to have the desire and the will to serve an ideal and to understand that, once elected, they belonged to the whole movement, not to one small part of it. They were expected to maintain their integrity in the face of undoubted temptations and not to deviate from the high standard of conduct required from a leader of the movement, for the Committee Man was, indeed, a leader in his society. He ought not to be 'on the Committee' because he thought being a Committee Man would give him greater standing in the community, or give him perks denied to others, or provide a useful stepping stone to another, higher office which was his ultimate goal. Nor was the office fulfilled by mere attendance at a certain number of meetings.

To 'get on the Committee' a candidate had to be nominated after which he stood for election. The poll was never high, just as attendance at the Annual General Meeting was never large. Having been elected to the Committee, the new member had to offer himself for re-election at regular intervals.

The Ashington Industrial Co-operative Society was a business, but it was a business with a difference. It was not concerned solely to make a profit for its shareholders (i.e. its members); it was concerned with the whole way of life and standard of living of these same shareholders. It was committed to the ideals of better conditions, better pay, less working hours and better housing for its members and employees.

Committee men were expected to attend the Annual Conference of the Co-operative Union. The Co-operative Union was, and is, the most comprehensive Federation in the movement and, therefore, was, and is, able to speak for the movement as a whole. Retail Societies and others paid a membership fee to the Union and were thereafter entitled to one vote per 1,000 members. Attendance at the Union's Annual Congress was limited to no more than six delegates per society. Congress, which took place early in Whit Week, was the annual meeting of members of the Union. The policy of the movement was moulded at this meeting which was world-wide in its scope. Delegates congregated from all parts of the world where the Co-op Union operated, and foreign delegates were invited to speak. It was an opportunity for Co-operators everywhere to meet, to exchange ideas, renew friendships and form new ones. It cemented the feeling of unity and good fellowship. In addition, the Union protected the interests of individual societies.

18. The Arcade

The episodes already mentioned did much towards making me accepted but there were things which still rankled, particularly with the older men.

First of all, there were the holidays. As a newcomer, I didn't merit a holiday until I had been with the Society for a year, after which my quota was one week, and, after further service, ten days. The majority of staff got ten days, from Monday till a week the following Friday. The weekend intervening was the old 'Baff Weekend' when things were supposed to be quieter and slacker. If they were, it was only marginally. Only one member of staff could be away at any one time and we shuffled around to fill in the gaps occasioned by our absentee.

To be absolutely fair to everyone, the Boss would tell us without batting an eyelid, the names were all put in a hat and taken out at random. He performed this act in the privacy of his home, burning the midnight oil while we enjoyed ourselves. It was a difficult task he had to do, but he didn't shirk it. We murmured various unintelligible things indicative of what a fine Boss we had and waited for him to produce the holiday list. Most of us could have written it beforehand with a 90 per cent chance of being absolutely right. Somehow, the apprentices always came out of the hat first and last. The two youngest apprentices got their holidays in March and the next two in November. Any left over and those just out of their time got April. In May and October came those who were out of favour, the oil man and the warehousemen together with the man who delivered groceries. June and September saw the less-favoured journeymen, the foreman and the bacon man. July and August saw the favourites and Rose Lynch.

'It's disappointing for some,' the Boss would say as he wrapped currants to show that he was at one with his staff and not above working with them, 'me included. The wife wanted

September. I wanted September. And, damn me if I didn't come out at the end of July. Sometimes, you know – I've seen it happen often – you get better weather in May and October than you get in July and August.' The apprentices' desire for holidays in the holiday months was beneath notice.

Thus, for me to claim a holiday in prime holiday time when I wasn't entitled to any holiday at all was an unpopular thing to do, to say the least. Not only that, but I'd be away two Saturdays, Baff and Pay. There was a general feeling, kept to mutterings intended for my ears, that I should forgo the Summer School Scholarship that occasioned my need for a week off work. Of course, as the store had awarded me this particular scholarship, they were hard pressed to say I couldn't go and I had no intention whatever of offering to give it up. I did have to do without pay, however. As I still had scholarships in hand, I was going to have to get time off for two further years, at least. This would have to be taken into consideration in future holiday lists. Manifestly, this was very unfair.

Having no school homework and an almost insatiable desire to learn, I started shorthand and typing lessons, as well as increasing the number of store classes I attended. The first lot of examination results to be published in the *Wheatsheaf* after I started work found my name at the top of the three lists in the examinations I had taken. I looked at these lists taking as much pleasure in what I read there as Sir Walter Elliot of Kellynch Hall in Somersetshire got from reading the Baronetage. One of the older men came along as I read the page yet again and I said, 'Look there.' He did not even glance to where I pointed.

He said, 'I don't care how many exams you sit, or how many you're top of, you'll never be anything more than what you are now – a counter-hand. It would do you far more good, if, instead of filling your head with that rubbish, you began to think about looking round for a decent steady lad. You're the sort that could get married at 19. You should be learning to look after a house for when you do get married or you'll find you'll be left with the cleft stick.'

I felt foolish. Snubbed. Abashed. Without answering, I got myself back to the little office and stood looking at the book I was working on without seeing it. My elation of a few moments ago had been completely vanquished. Apart from feeling humiliated, I felt totally confused. How could anything so obviously worth congratulation, at least, be disapproved of? And I couldn't explain why, but I felt trapped and an anger was rising within me and the not knowing why made it worse.

At school, examination results were all-important. To get a high mark meant, automatically, you'd worked hard; to come in the middle – satisfactory; to be bottom, or nearly bottom – you obviously had made no effort or worse. In this case, I'd worked for recognition, not for any reward that might accrue. I so much wished to be considered as capable as they, that I even wore collars and ties most of the time, though I much prefer less regimental clothes. What was wrong? It was almost the same on the books. I took as much pride as Mr Routh in getting all my totals right and practised long and hard to try and achieve this end.

Bobby did most of the checking and when he found no mistakes in one of Mr Routh's books, he would say, 'Not a mistake there, Alf. Every one right. Your books don't need checking.'

And Mr Routh, obviously pleased at what Bobby had said, would reply modestly, 'Oh. It all comes with practice, lad.'

As I stood totalling next to Bobby while he checked mine, I'd be aware of whether or not he was changing a figure, or merely initialling. On one occasion, I was sure they were all correct; he made no comment, so I said, 'I'll take that book straight to Rose, if you like.' In Rose's office, squashed up against her coat, I licked through the total end of each page. I had been right. Not one total had been corrected.

Back in the office, I said in an offhand way, 'Did you find any mistakes in that book, Bobby?'

'I'm here to do a job, not to count your mistakes,' he replied.

The remark concerning the examination results had several facets which I could not then see. A great many agreed with the speaker and did think I was wasting my time going to classes. His tone was probably dictatorial and scathing because he was saying something that 'had to be said'. I couldn't get any promotion, no matter how hard I worked. The apprentices and journeymen, those who had started in the store before they were 16, would be promoted in the fulness of time in the order in which they had first started work, regardless of whether they'd done well or not at the apprentices' classes. Thus, I was wasting my time. No one considered that I might want knowledge for its own sake.

Also, the business of a young girl was to get a decent lad, get married and give up any job she had. She was then expected to clean, cook, wash and scrub for her husband and family. If I went on in this foolish way, I might miss out on the matrimonial stakes altogether. No lad wanted a wife whose head was full of books, who couldn't (or didn't) knit, embroider or give any evidence that she knew how to make a leek pudding or the like. Worse, as far as these stakes were concerned, I might get so above myself that no lad would be good enough for me.

The one thing that had to be prevented at all costs was allowing anyone to become swollen-headed. Success might mean you got above yourself, a state of affairs not to be tolerated. Thus, praise was hardly ever given or, on the rare occasions when it was forthcoming in modified form, it was always accompanied by a little homily on the merits of hard work and not forgetting who you were or what you were.

So that, really, our lines of communication were crossed. The more they tried to discourage me from aping them and their jobs as grocers and behave as a young girl should, the more I thought they disapproved of me because I didn't measure up to their standards as grocers and the harder I tried.

As so often happens, the results were not what I set out to achieve, but they were beneficial to me in the long run, though I had to wait years before I saw this. It left me with one attitude, however, that I could not shake off for much of my 'official' working life. It was that, just to stay equal, I had to work ten times harder than anyone else. I never dreamed of saying 'No' to any job, even when the asking was an imposition. This was particularly true if the person making the request happened to be a man. I held this attitude long after I'd learned that although others' assessment of me was important, my assessment of myself was just as important; long after I'd learned to listen carefully to what was said on any given point or circumstance, to modify my attitude if I thought it right but, having come to a decision or viewpoint on the situation, to stick to that decision even in the face of opposition.

All things considered, then, as far as work was concerned I left for my summer school in a somewhat sullen atmosphere. On my return I was agreeably surprised to find that complaints about my lack of usefulness and ineptitude had gone. It was many years before, inadvertently, I found out the reason for this.

On the Thursday evening, the Boss had called the men together after the shop shut and said, in effect, 'I don't want to hear any more complaints about that lass. The only thing I ever hear is, she can't do this and she can't do that. She's no use. This week we've seen different. She works hard and she's been missed. Think on what I've said. That's all.'

More and more, especially with the apprentices and the younger men, I was becoming one of them. For a while, I severed my allegiance with my Ashington friends and struck up a friendship with a girl from Newbiggin. This was, in part, cupboard love: I'd seen a tall, handsome Romeo on the promenade and he knew my friend and sometimes stopped to talk with us. This liaison was having a disastrous effect on my pocket money. One Friday, when the shop was full, I was surprised to see this new girl friend standing at the back of the line of waiting customers. Dressed in her Sunday coat, she gesticulated that she wanted to talk to me. The Boss was standing on the steps of his eyrie, his all-seeing eye on his underlings. I chose a well-known 'canny body' for my next customer in spite of protests that others had waited longer, signalled my friend with my eyes, and disappeared behind the cheese counter. Here, for a few seconds, I was safe.

I seized the cheese knife and a bit of American cheese purposefully and hissed to my friend, 'Why have you got your Sunday coat on?'

'I'm going out with a lad.'

'Does your mother know?'

'No to both. Listen. You-know-who is going to wait outside to walk you home when the shop closes. I told him eight o'clock.' A loud coughing and throat-clearing indicated that the Boss was making his way counterwards. I fled back to my customer agog with suppressed excitement.

As eight o'clock approached I went as near the plate-glass window as I dared and peered out into the darkened street. Yes. There he was on the edge of the pavement, the image of a film star with his Robert Colman moustache, his trilby hat on at an angle, his belted coat with the collar turned up and his new gloves that he got for Christmas. My maiden heart beat as if it were a sledgehammer and I was like to swoon for very joy . . . except that there were still customers to be served – and with increased speed, if they were to be got out of the shop by five past eight at the latest.

Like a film star . . .

At six minutes past eight, I detached myself from the group as we came out of the shop and walked up to my handsome hero, my legs like jelly. We said rather self-conscious 'hellos' and he took off his glove and put his hand in his pocket.

'I've brought you a few sweets,' he said as he handed me a small bagful.

'Oh, thank you,' I breathed as though they were the largest box of the most expensive handmade chocolates instead of satin mixtures already clagging to the bag.

We set off walking in the direction of my home. As we approached the Grand Corner we crossed the road and I was somewhat surprised to see two of the apprentices coming towards us. One cannoned into me.

'I'm terribly sorry, Miss,' he said. Then, 'Oh. It's you. I thought it was a young lady. Fancy me making a mistake like that.' This last remark was addressed to two young men from the shop walking almost on our heels. Under normal circumstances I would have found it difficult enough to carry on a conversation, but now it was almost impossible as I strained to hear what was being said behind my back, tried to get away from those saying it and, at the same time, appear to my escort as if nothing was wrong.

'What time do they expect you at home?' he asked.

'Well,' I said, as carelessly as I could, 'when I come. I mean, I can please myself.' (Actually, ten o'clock was the absolute deadline.)

We went for a short walk, but I was hardly conscious of where we went, what with one thing and another. Every corner we turned, we bumped into one couple or the other of our four bloodhounds. At last we returned to the fence at Booth's Corner, the side away from the road. This was as far as I could go in safety because I wasn't yet considered old enough to have a lad. We chose one of the little pools of shadow created by the single light in its vain attempt to illuminate the whole area. Hardly had we stopped than another couple stopped also. From the other end of the fence, a second couple appeared.

'Been for a walk?' the first couple shouted.

'Yes,' the second called back. 'I was just saying old men that go out with young girls get on my wick.'

'Me as well. Especially committeemen's daughters.'

'Yes. Them that have stern parents.'

I blushed in the semi-darkness. My father had put up for the store committee shortly after I became employed there and was voted on. The next morning the apprentices had got me at the cheese counter and said, 'What's he like, your Old Man? Him that's now a committeeman. What sort of a father is he?'

I was still at the rookie stage, grateful for any little attention. To have four of them, hanging on to any reply I was going to make, unbalanced me completely.

'He's . . . he's a stern parent,' I had stammered, and regretted what I'd said the moment I'd said it, but it was too late. (I didn't mean what I said. My father was a gentle and extremely kind man, conscientious and honest to an almost painful degree and very anxious that, through hard work, my brother and I should do well.)

They had hooted with laughter and joyfully spread the news round the shop.

'Did you hear that? Our new committeeman is a stern parent.'

'We'll have to watch out now. We have a stern parent on the committee,' and so on and so forth. *Ad infinitum. Ad nauseam.*

I said goodnight to my swain, having promised to see him next night after work.

'He's too old for you,' they said next morning when I got to the shop.

'He's only 22.'

'Haddaway. He's an old man. He's 24 if he's a day.'

'He's a right cissie, too. He wears gloves!' This was considered the height of effeminacy. In even the coldest and bleakest weather no man, if he was a man, wore gloves.

'And he wears a hat!'

'James Cagney wears a hat,' I said. It was a mistake. All that day, when we were not under the immediate eye of the Boss or the foreman, one or other would adopt a James Cagney stance, putting his hands out in front, shaking them and saying, 'Yuh got it comin' to yuh, kid. Sweeties.' Or, 'OK. Stick 'em up.' Then, lisping, 'Don't be afraid. It's only a chocolate gun with sweets inside.'

Or they minced up with an effete droop of the wrist and said, 'I've brought you some sweeties.'

At that, another one would get down on his knees and say, looking up, 'Oh, thank you, thank you,' and kiss his feet.

At half-past seven, I again separated myself from the group and went up to the young man standing at the edge of the pavement. I looked at him and, behold, my hero of 24 hours ago was nowhere in evidence. Before me stood a very ordinary young man whose company I now no longer sought.

One of our teachers at what were called the apprentices' classes was also a colleague. His name was Billy Ruddick. He was well liked, conscientious and desirous, however unpromising the material, of having his students pass their examinations in book-keeping, the Co-operative variety. Why they should have had to toil thus I do not know, for no one I knew actually used this method of book-keeping. There were three stages. No one really reckoned on getting through Stage One at the first attempt. And for some, it took three attempts. There were those who made Stage One last their whole apprenticeship.

But Billy never gave up hope and to augment his Wednesday afternoon class, he had a few of us at his home on Sunday mornings. I must add that apprentices from other Societies joined the Ashington classes.

I loved these Sunday mornings. It wasn't just the lesson; I loved being there. I wore my best clothes and got out of helping with the Sunday lunch, the most laborious meal of the week. I was the only girl among six students, one of whom was a tall, good-looking lad from another Society. He was nicknamed 'Big Mitch' and appeared much more sophisticated than we.

One Wednesday we went on an 'educational trip' to the CWS factories on the Tyne and arrived back in Newcastle in the early evening with our return train tickets and sundry samples from the factories among which was a large packet of CWS cornflakes. The company broke up and Big Mitch went to meet his girlfriend while four of us decided to go to the pictures at the Stoll; at 15 I'd never yet been to a Newcastle cinema. Had I fancied any one of the three lads more than any other, we might have split into two groups, but I liked them all equally.

After the pictures, we had fish and chips and then went for the train. We had a carriage to ourselves. Before long, the place was awash with cornflakes as we pelted each other with them, pushed them down each other's necks, kicked and struggled to avoid being scrubbed by them till, eventually, we reached our home station. It was, perhaps, a sad waste of cornflakes, especially at that time, but Freud, did he know about the incident, would probably disagree.

One day, some time after this incident, Jimmy Hall, one of the apprentices, lured me to the cheese counter and said, 'Big Mitch wants to know if he asked you to go out with him, would you go?'

'Tell Big Mitch,' I said with a toss of the head that I hoped made me look like Bette Davis, 'that I don't go out with lads that go out with other girls.'

'You don't want to be so high and mighty, hoying your head up like that. Just come off your high horse. If you don't go out with Big Mitch, there's plenty that will. You'll not do any better. I know the Stern Parent has a good job at the pit' – he meant he was on an upstanding wage – 'and he's a committeeman but Big Mitch's folks have *money*. And I mean money. His Old Man married into money. Her mam has at least three houses that I know of and they'll get the lot when she snuffs it. So stop hoying your head up in that daft way or you'll end up in the clarts.'

This was very sound advice, but I kept Bette Davis in mind and, with another haughty toss of the head, said, 'I am not in the least influenced by what you say,' and made my exit. I *was* interested, of course. Tremendously.

Two days later I was again summoned to the cheese counter with a conspiratorial jerk of the head.

'Big Mitch says he's finished with his lass. He says, if he goes to the Arcade on Saturday will you be there. He says, if you are and he asks you to dance, will you get up with him.'

That I remembered Bette Davis at all at such a time speaks volumes for the impact she made on me.

'Tell Big Mitch,' I said with half-open eyes and sulky mouth, 'I'll think about it.'

'You'd better be there,' he said. 'I've told him you will and that you'll dance with him, so think on.'

I couldn't think of any suitable reply other than another toss of the head and a dramatic exit to the back shop *à la* Bette Davis.

'You don't half look daft when you walk like that,' he shouted after me.

Actually, I was overwhelmed at the small triumph that lay ahead, nay, two small triumphs.

Generally speaking, girls had to be 17 before they were allowed to go out with a lad or bring one home. This did not mean we never went out with lads before we were given the go-ahead, but it did give added spice and daring to what was probably ordinary and mundane.

I had just celebrated my sixteenth birthday when, to my complete surprise, my mother said, 'Your father and I have been talking and we think that, now you're growing up and acting responsibly, if you meet a lad and he asks you to go out with him, you can – but, first, you have to bring him home so that we can meet him. If you're going out with some lad and you don't want to bring him home to let us see him, or he doesn't want to come, there's something wrong and you should give him up.'

Now, gratifying though this news was, it had its negative side. It was one thing to be told you could have a lad, it was another thing to realize there was no lad, either on hand or in the offing.

And now, this.

Also, the Arcade was the Society's ball-room in their Hirst premises. Every Wednesday and Saturday they held a dance there with a dance band. Three members of the band were brothers, one of whom worked in the grocery department. I was going to say 'with me' but, somehow, this elevates my position too much.

Every Wednesday evening the Society held a dancing class from seven till eight. There may have been one on a Saturday night also, but if there was I wouldn't know. We worked till seven-thirty.

I had attended the Wednesday Night Learners' Class. They were run by the long-time girlfriend of the eldest brother of the band trio, so I was told. Of course, the band did not play for the learners' class. Music was provided by a gramophone, asthmatic in its senility. The few records used were out-dated and heavily overworked. The burden of their years had taken its toll. We assembled, the girls on one side of the hall, the boys on the other. Not all the dancing teacher's cajoling or ordering could make us intermingle. French chalk had been laid down to facilitate our movements. Our teacher stood at the top of the hall and placed a large card on an easel. The card stated, in bold letters, 'MODERN WALTZ'. We always started with a modern waltz. For those who could not read, or didn't trouble to, she announced that this dance would be a modern waltz and executed (an apt word) a few steps indicative of the gentleman's part and the same steps in reverse to show us how the ladies should dance.

'Now, boys,' she said, 'go up to the girls and do remember to say, "May I have the pleasure of this dance, please?" '

Nobody moved. The boys who had been addressed looked from one to the other to see who was going to be brave enough to take the first step. Finally, one did and the most courageous of those remaining followed suit. It was an agonizing moment for us girls. Would we be among the last to be picked, or, humiliation upon humiliation, would we be in a position where the teacher would take a boy who had rejected those remaining and *make* him say the words to claim us as a partner?

In this latter respect, I was lucky; I was not brought to the final humiliation. A small lad, about 14 years of age, ill at ease in his Sunday suit, stood before me. He jerked his head.

'Howway,' he said.

'You're not supposed to say that,' I admonished. 'You're supposed to say, "May I have the pleasure?" ' I really meant this as a joke.

'Are you coming, or have I to ask somebody else?'

In reply, I put my hands on his shoulders.

'Wait till we get to the middle,' he said irritably. When we had walked a few steps towards the centre, we put our hands on each other's shoulders and waited. Satisfied that her brood was in a state of mind conducive to instruction, the teacher repeated the information that this was a modern waltz and recalled for our benefit the steps we should use. She walked over to the gramophone, wound it up, applied the needle, the instrument creaked and scratched into action and a querulous voice wondered for the thousandth time why Charmaine kept him waiting. We might have told him why, but the teacher quickly overpowered his brooding entreaties. ONE two three. ONE two three. NOTSUCHBIGSTEPS two three. ONE two three. ONE two three. HANDSONEACHOTHERSSHOULDERS two three. ONE two three. ONE two three. YOUGOFORWARD two three. SHEGOESBACK two three. ONE two three. It was difficult to hear the rheumaticky plaintive gramophone. The teacher's voice, the sliding feet of the would-be dancers just off-beat, the heavy breathing of Youth concentrating on its feet filled the hall. When, in the course of the dance, we got to the bottom of the hall, we had to rely on the counting. We couldn't hear the music at all. Even if there had been no other distracting sounds it couldn't be heard.

'Don't you think,' I said to my partner, 'we should hold each other the proper way? I've never seen any couples dance like this. Shouldn't we try the proper way?'

'I've come here to learn to dance,' my partner replied chivalrously, 'not to waste time talking. I wish I had asked somebody else now. I can't stand people who yap away all the time, especially when I'm concentrating.'

We continued shuffling around. The gradual, uncertain cessation of sliding feet and the absence of any counting led us to suppose the record had finished and the dance was over.

'No. No. No.' It was the teacher's voice again. She never gave up. 'Take your partner's arm, guide her back to her seat and say, "Thank you".'

My partner took my arm and pushed me in the general direction of the 'girls' wall'. 'Ta,' he said self-consciously, ashamed of this slight defection from his manhood.

The teacher changed the board and the record. She returned to the easel and in the desperate tones of an Infants teacher with a hopeless class pointed to the words and said, 'This is a fox trot.' The lesson continued.

As eight o'clock approached, the members of the band made their mournful way to the stage and began setting up their instruments. There was a slight lull to mark the end of the class and, during this time, more French chalk was scattered over the floor. Then the band, with what appeared to be great vexation of spirit, took over and played the music for a 'progressive' or 'Bradford' barn dance. It was the wallflowers' very last chance of a positive dance that night. The MC made *all* the men stand up.

If you didn't come to the dance in time to take part in the 'Bradford' then you'd really arrived. You could afford to come late, secure in the knowledge that you either had a partner already or were sure of having an ample supply when you got there. The following Wednesday night, I was going to join that élite body, thanks to the good offices of Jimmy and the presence of Big Mitch. For those who like the ends of their stories neatly tied up, Big Mitch became my first official boyfriend but the liaison did not last long.

The Arcade was used for other things besides the weekly hop. Sometimes, on a Sunday, the store band (orchestra) gave a concert. In season, the annual dances of many of the local groups and Societies were held there, usually on a Friday night, although the store usually gave its dance on a Wednesday night, thus stopping that night's hop. For some reason, the hospital and the store had an annual 'dance' but the rotary and the police had an annual 'ball'.

The Co-op Players also used the hall on a Wednesday and a Saturday night three times a year when they put on a play. Usually, they filled the hall on four consecutive nights on these occasions. Even the advent of regular picture-going did not lessen the allegiance and loyalty to the Players. I joined and, like all aspiring junior thespians, I began at the bottom selling programmes. Before I'd served my apprenticeship in this field, the war was upon us and we were converted into a sort of ENSA group formed to entertain the troops. My part in these shows was as a singing and dancing girl, one of those who came on at the beginning and first after the interval. I was totally miscast. It must have been a great relief to everyone, players and audience alike, when I left to serve King and Country.

I had not been at shorthand and typing long before the teacher thought I should aim for some other job, which meant that I should try to get into an office. As luck would have it, a month or two later, when I had my first certificates in each subject, a vacancy did occur in the store general office, the large open-plan building situated in the centre of the blocks of shops and offices at the top of the wide, sweeping marble-like staircase. There was only one course open to me, my shorthand teacher said, I must apply. My letter of application met with her seal of approval and to it she added a glowing testimonial. I kept all this information to myself, an unnecessary thing to do.

'I hear,' said George Wade to me one Thursday morning as we prepared for the onslaught of customers, 'you've applied for that job in the office. Well, you're wasting your time. *You're* not going to get it.'

'Do you know who is?'

'No. I only know you're not.'

'The shorthand teacher says I should stand a very good chance.'

'I don't care what she says, you're not going to get it, so just make your mind up to it.'

There wasn't much time for further conversation. Later, when I'd been banished to the office to start on books, Jack McKenzie came in.

'That office job,' he said, keeping his eye on the approaches through a slit between the biscuit tins, 'you don't really want it, do you? I can't think what made you apply. You'll hardly be any better-off. All you'll get out of it is a Saturday afternoon off. It's not worth it. It's not half as nice working up there as it is here. There's no fun up there. It's like a morgue. There'll be no stopping for gossips there. Everybody looking at you all the time. You've even got to ask permission to go to the cloakroom there, I'm told, and then you're timed. I mean, how often do you see them laugh while they're up there working? And how many office lasses come down here for three penn'orth of biscuits and a bit of squeeze? Give it up. Tell them you don't want the job. You'll regret it if you don't. Think on, now.'

Jack had put into words what I had been thinking in a confused sort of way. I'd been flattered beyond measure when the shorthand teacher had spoken to me about the job in the first place and, somehow, I felt I couldn't not apply. Indeed, for what other reason was I doing shorthand and typing if I didn't want an office job? After Jack had gone, I realized I really didn't want to move. I did like my job. More, I was really beginning to enjoy the work. But, in the face of what she'd said on the subject, how could I tell all this to the shorthand teacher, especially after what she'd written about me. In any case, I had no idea how to set about saying I wanted to withdraw my application. And, in spite of what Jack had said, I might like the job, if I got it. I hadn't thought much of this one at the beginning. I had no real confidence in George's pronouncements. My faith was in the teacher.

Saturday afternoons and evenings had a vaguely Saturn alian air. The next day, Sunday was a day of rest from work, and the evening in between, socially speaking, was the highlight of the week. There were those of more sophisticated taste and greater affluence who might go as far afield as Newcastle for their weekend entertainment, but most stayed in either Ashington or Hirst, both of which bid fair to cater for all tastes. There were four cinemas, the Regal, the Buff (Buffalo) the Waller (Wallow), the Piv (Pavilion). Each would have changed to a new film on Thursday and each would have two houses. To be sure of getting a seat at the second house of any of these cinemas on a Saturday night, it was best to book. Also, there were, I'm told, 34 working-men's clubs at that time, together with two hotels/public houses, the Grand and the Portland. There were two major dance halls, the Arcade and the Princess Ballroom as well as the Harmonic Hall and sundry church halls often given over to dances and socials. And there were whist drives. All of these venues were filled to near bursting-point on a Saturday night.

A young blade might go to the first-house pictures, go for a pint and finish up at one of the dance halls where he might 'click' (i.e. get himself a young lady). Even for those who attended none of these things, it was a night for visiting. Even the customers who came into the shop on a Saturday night to pay their bills did so as part of the evening's entertainment and wore, not the coat they kept for the store, but their second best. Mothers came with grown-up daughters and younger daughters and married sisters came together. They would leave the store to walk 'down the street' and look at the shops and, perhaps, walk through

Woolworth's before going back home for a bite of supper before the men came in from the club. They usually visited the store first because it was the first to close. Most shops stayed open till nine and some were open even later. Very often, some of the younger married men were met by their wives and children after they came out of the shop that they might go for some treat before they all went home.

Usually, all the staff changed into different clothes on a Saturday lunch-time, when we didn't close but had a staggered break. All the coats and aprons were pristine white, almost shining, on Friday and Saturday nights. This was the time for changing into freshly laundered 'whites'. Only the Boss and Rose came into the shop without a coat. The warehousemen wore tan overalls.

There was almost a jocular atmosphere. The work of the week was over; the orders up and out and the money collected in, the shop busy and the week's takings up to scratch. The Boss usually came out of his office and joined those putting up sugar or something similar at the first counter. I usually worked with the second counter-hand serving and, in the lull periods, putting up small quantities of things like ground almonds which came in a fairly small box, not a sack.

This Saturday it was different. There was a restraint and a silence in the shop which I found difficult to understand. I had a feeling that something was afoot and everybody knew about it but I, a not uncommon state of affairs. Another odd thing was happening. George and I were putting up glacé cherries, a sticky job. A scoop was available but George always used his hands. He said it was better that way, he didn't have to wash the scoop afterwards. He didn't add that neither did he have to serve customers – his hands being so sticky, so I did all the serving necessary. Today, he was using a scoop. Not only that, often, when a customer came in, he would tell me it was all right, I could carry on with what I was doing, he would serve. It was not only puzzling, it was worrying. Such considerate behaviour aroused my suspicions. The Boss didn't put in an appearance either; he stayed in his office.

Presently, a committeeman appeared. He walked straight

through to the Boss's office. There was nothing unusual about that even if we'd known he was coming. A few minutes later, they both came out. The Boss nodded towards Mr Routh who laid his scoop on the counter and walked in line with the two men, he on one side of the counter, they on the other. They met up at the opening leading to the back shop, turned right and went down the stone steps and no remarks were made about what they were likely to be doing there, another unusual thing.

Work continued for some time and still the three men had not reappeared from the cellar. General conversation began in a muted, modified way, but stopped when there were noises indicating that the absentees were returning. Mr Routh came up first more red-faced than usual. He returned to his place and the man who had been 'filling' handed over the scoop. The Boss and the committeeman, in the meantime, disappeared into the office. The Boss carried with him an old order book. Mr Routh was a trifle put out. Angry even, although he was doing his best to conceal it, as he often did, but his ruddy cheeks and glinting spectacle frames gave his mood away, as they often did.

'You found it then?' said the foreman.

'I'm here to do what I'm told,' Mr Routh said testily.

There was a difference between him and The Raj and the rest of the staff. I was given to understand that both of these gentlemen had been managers of other grocery shops which had closed when their firms had fallen on lean times. They'd been given a job in the store on the understanding that, for them, there would be no further promotion. The Boss treated them both with respect, as did the rest of the staff. The Boss was more at home with Mr Routh, who must have been nearing retirement age when I was there. For Mr Routh it no doubt rankled that he now had to take orders when once he had been used to giving them. The Raj, on the other hand, was a different kettle of fish. He remained aloof from it all. He served customers at his own pace, and, if he felt disposed to chat with them, he did so, whether or not we were busy. He did not trouble to discern who was next when he was serving, but served the person nearest to 'his place' on the counter. He also served any customer whom he felt should not be kept waiting, regardless of whether it was her turn or not. When there was a lull in customers, he did not help to put up stock. Instead, he took his pencil from behind his ear, looked at it and replaced it more firmly. With two hands, he carefully slid out his till (the drawer model with the space at the back for notes and little wooden bowls for copper and silver) and scrutinized its contents. He stirred the various denominations of coins up in their little wooden bowls, lifted the bowl containing the silver out and looked at the notes which had been hidden underneath. He counted them slowly and carefully, making each look the same way, separated the tens from the ones, dadded them on the counter to make a neat rectangular pile of each, slowly replaced them, returned the 'silver' compartment, stirred up the copper and slowly and carefully slid the drawer back to close the till. If there were still no customers, he would scrutinize every area of the shop in turn, lastly looking the shelves over. He had a way of being able to spin this out to fill the time available. Occasionally, he sent an apprentice for a crate of milk (the tinned variety) and asked him to open it. It rarely got as far as that, and if it did, only on Tuesdays did he go any further.

The Boss, who was often irritated by this slow motion, never spoke to him directly. Instead, he made general statements in a loud voice about the need for speedy serving on the counter with no gossiping. It fell on the deaf ears of the only person for whom it was intended.

However, this afternoon, there was no Boss to watch his counter-hand's slow-motion activities. He stayed with the committeeman and the book they'd brought from the cellar, closeted in his office. Presently, there was a lot of purposeful activity. The Boss opened his door and the two men came noisily from the office, the Boss leading.

'Here,' he said to The Raj who was gazing into his till, 'take pay for some tobacco. It's been missed off the order.' Everyone's eyes were turned to look at this transaction, while The Raj obeyed with greater alacrity than was usual. I was puzzled. I did not know how this could possibly be. I, myself, had extended and totalled his bill this week and the tobacco had been most certainly charged for. We all knew about the committeemen who dealt with us and we were most careful to see that their bills were absolutely correct. This tobacco was a known pitfall. It was not a popular brand and it wasn't ordered regularly. Thus the order man did not know whether we'd have any in stock or not. If we didn't, another brand would have to be sent. Consequently, the amount was often left out. The order men only left amounts off their bills for unusual circumstances. Normally, they filled their own prices in, but they still had to be checked. The Raj had to make out a yellow check as the committeeman did not have his check book with him. Finally, the transaction was completed and the Boss walked with his visitor to the door.

'I'm sorry,' said the committeeman so that we could all hear, 'but I felt I had to come.'

'You only did what was right,' the Boss replied and, having seen his visitor off the premises (another unusual thing) he returned to his exalted cubicle nodding a message to the foreman as he mounted the steps and closed the door. By a turn of the head, the foreman bounced the message from his head to that of George with whom I was working.

'Boss wants to see you,' that gentleman said to me, correctly decoding the wordless signal.

Totally perplexed I walked to the presence-chamber, knocked and was told to come in. The Boss was sitting sideways on his desk on which lay an opened book. An order book.

'Close the door, hinny,' he said. I already had and was standing at as respectful a distance from him as his cramped quarters would allow.

'I'm awful sorry about this, hinny, but you've been a bit careless. If it had been anybody else it wouldn't have mattered so much, but you've never charged a committeeman for some tobacco.' (He called it 'baccy'.)

'Oh, but I did charge Sir,' I said this last word in considerably less than a whisper. I had already learned this much, at least. He liked to be called 'Sir'. Not for worlds would I have had anyone hear me utter that servile word, however. 'I can tell you how much it was. I remember writing it. I do distinctly.'

'Now, hinny,' he said. 'Don't get yourself upset. I wasn't talking about this week, nor last week neither. Look. There it is. You can see for yourself.'

I looked and recognized from the poor figuring in the total which had been wrong in the shillings column and had been changed, that this was the work I had done nearly two years previously when I first started extending. Now, my figuring flowed more smoothly and I took as much pride in not missing a price and having all-correct totals as either of my two colleagues.

'It was carelessness, hinny. You can't say anything else. I did what I could to speak up for you but this sort of thing costs the Society money. A lot of money.' He sucked his teeth and shook his head. My mouth was dry and I couldn't speak. His kindness in the face of my mistake, his admission that he had done his best for me could only mean one thing. I was to be sacked. 'So you see, I couldn't honestly recommend you, now could I? If you were to get that job in the general office a mistake like that might cost the Society hundreds. They deal in big figures, not little ones like this. You couldn't expect anybody to take that risk, could you?'

So that was it! It wasn't the sack. It was the office job. Relief flooded over me so that I was no more capable of speech then than I had been earlier.

'You do understand, now, don't you hinny? And there's no hard feelings? I did my best, but the evidence was there.'

I nodded. It was all I could manage. I went back to the shop. I'd have loved to have blurted out my joy that I needn't worry about whether or not I got the office job any more. It was settled. The decision had been taken out of my hands. But the atmosphere in the shop was still subdued and the reason for it still eluded me. I went straight to the end of the counter where we were putting up cherries. George was serving and making a meal of it. Another customer came in and I made to go forward, but he said it was all right; he would serve.

I wrapped the remaining cherries. The rhythmic movement was soothing and I began to think more calmly. I would give up shorthand and typing. Somehow, I didn't want to tell the teacher what had happened. In any case, if I carried on, there might be more office jobs and I wanted to stay here. I packed the cherries into a box and, as I did so, it seemed that a dark shadow moved swiftly and disappeared under the counter. I put both hands on the counter and looked down trying to work out what it was that I'd seen, or thought I'd seen. If it was a mouse, the shop cats would be in trouble. They existed solely to keep the mice down. If it was a mouse they would be denied their weekly meal of raw meat which came from the butchery department just before closing time. They were fed this by Jimmy, who obviously thought he was feeding the big cats at the zoo. He snarled as he threw the meat at them and growled to try to imitate what he thought they did when they were fed. He looked upon this as one of the perks of his job and kept it when it ought to have gone to his junior. As I stood wondering, Jack came up and put his hand on my shoulder.

'Hold your head up, pet,' he said. 'You've come out of this with your colours flying.'

I looked up and did what I so much wanted to do. I smiled. I hadn't the least idea of what he was talking about but I did realize his tone was congratulatory. I had noticed this sort of thing before and was to notice it again. I often did something which I thought merited praise, or at least recognition, but none was forthcoming; then I'd be praised when, in my estimation, I'd done nothing praiseworthy. I learned to make the most of these puzzling situations and work a system of balances.

Out of gratitude to Jack, I forbore to mention the fact that I thought I'd seen a mouse and thus I did not deprive the cats of their Saturday-night banquet or Jimmy of his intrepid encounter with the snarling wildlife of his invention.

19. Eat What Ye Like

The Boss's instruction on my first morning that I could eat what I liked in the shop was, in fact, a good one, although it was one that I could not take advantage of for some time, much as I wanted to. I was far too timid and far too concerned with trying to please and keep track of all the things I was supposed to know to have courage enough to eat the chocolate and sweets that tempted me sorely. My eating something from the shop was made the more difficult because most of the others rarely ate anything from stock at all, and, when they did, it was usually a piece of cheese which they consumed rather as one concerned with its taste and texture, as if it was being eaten in the course of duty rather than because of a selfish, personal desire. This also went for a new variety of biscuits or chocolate. They were sampled from the Boss down, everyone giving the impression that it was the quality of the tit-bit in question that was being assessed, not the pleasure it gave to the individual palate. It was not uncommon for those of us who were serving to offer a customer a piece of cheese or a biscuit to sample when she was deliberating which kind of cheese, if any, or which variety of biscuit she was going to buy. We also frequently offered a biscuit or a sweet to very young children who had come shopping with their mother.

As I grew in confidence in the work I was doing, so the chocolate, sweets and biscuits grew in magnetism and one day I found myself standing next to an opened box of 2 d. bars of Cadbury's chocolate with no one near me and no one concerned with what I was doing. I whipped a bar into my pocket, hardly able to believe my luck.

I was sent down to the cellar for some reason or other and while I was there I crammed the chocolate into my mouth and gulped it down. Feeling and looking extremely guilty, I returned to the shop, but no one noticed anything out of the ordinary. Thereafter, I gave full reign to my sweet tooth.

The bacon counter held no attractions for me because I've never cared much for meat in any form. Crumbly Cheshire cheese I learned to like, as long as it was between two cream crackers liberally spread with butter. My favourite biscuits were Locarno Creams and Garden Creams and these I consumed in prodigious quantities. To this end, I placed either tin (or caused someone else to place either tin) immediately in front of the missing pane of glass above the bench in the little office. Thus I was able to do my books and dip my hand into the tin.

Liquorice all-sorts and coconut daisies were also among my favourites and it was rare for me not to have a handful of either in my overall pocket to sweeten my labours. Accordingly, at this time, my jaws scarcely ceased to move.

This state of affairs finally came to a head on Bank Holiday. My friend Joyce and I were each possessed of bikes and it was our intention to cycle to Rothbury for there Joyce intended to keep a tryst with a young man. Boy friends were still taboo but Joyce's friend and his friend were camping at Rothbury and they had asked us there for the day.

'Don't bring a thing,' we were told. 'It's to be our treat. We have a list of menus for the day and they're to be a surprise.'

I was extremely dubious. Not that I doubted their ability to cook. It was my capricious appetite I was worried about. To this end, before we left the shop on the Saturday, I asked Jack if I could have a shilling's worth (two-thirds of my pocket money at the time) of chocolate biscuits with as many of the round ones in as he could manage. He gave me a generous bagful with all the round ones left in the tin. I intended to keep the biscuits as a surprise, but I must confess that I really wanted to make sure there was at least one dish on the menu that I could eat with enjoyment.

I didn't mention the biscuits to Joyce and put them among all the other bits and pieces I was taking. We had hardly left the confines of Ashington when there, standing by the roadside with his bike, was Joyce's boyfriend.

We had arranged to meet him just outside Rothbury, but, such was his ardour, that, having been deprived of the sight of his adored one for something like 40 hours, he could not wait one second longer than was necessary. Their reunion after such an aeon of time was rapturous and prolonged. I was the look-out and retired to a convenient spot at a little distance to keep vigilance while they looked into each other's eyes, exclaiming at the abyss of time that had creaked by while an uncaring world had kept them apart. To help fill my lonely occupation, I fished out a biscuit – one of the round ones. Then I fished out another. When we recommenced our journey I kept a discreet distance from the two lovers, sussing out the environment as we went along. It was difficult. The roads were virtually deserted. It was a rotten sort of morning, cold, with rain threatening every minute. There wasn't much on apart from a few all-weather cyclists who saw only the road and the rear end of the person in front. As the first Rothbury houses came into view, I reached for another biscuit. The bag was empty.

When we reached the campsite the other member of the foursome was absolutely furious. He'd had to wrestle with the cooking of the midday meal himself. A fretful Primus held a pan of potatoes. A reluctant fire held a tin of peas among its ashes and, where the flames were, was a blackened frying pan containing four chops so charred as to be hardly distinguishable from their receptacle. The potatoes were hard, the peas cold and the chops black on the outside and red-raw within. Even had they been the result of Cordon Bleu cooking, I doubt whether I could have eaten them. My love-lorn companions had sensibilities only for each other and noticed nothing wrong, neither with the meal nor with the other male in the group who, in his turn, was solely occupied with his murderous thoughts. I spent the time surreptitiously disposing of the food on my plate. I slid the chop behind a convenient tuft of grass, sprinkled the peas on the ground and the more obvious potatoes I squashed into a pocket. The sweet was a lemon jelly, which had been put in a cool place to set. A cat had tested its surface as a possible skating rink and walked all over it. At least, I gave it as my opinion that it was a cat. I didn't want to think of the possibility of any other animal being in the vicinity.

The boys cleaned up the cooking utensils by sticking the cutlery in the ground and rubbing everything else with grass. The best they could rise to was tepid tea whose surface was awash with buoyant tea-leaves.

Our two captives of Cupid crawled into the tent. I and the boy remaining each went for a walk in opposite directions. All I wanted was to be alone to wrestle with the turmoil mounting with me. My stomach had been transformed into a cauldron of aggressive factions of chocolate that twisted and turned and fought for supremacy. The smell of chocolate became a stench blocking my nostrils, the taste of it clogged my mouth. Not for years had I eaten anything else but chocolate. I closed my eyes and chocolate biscuits of all shapes and sizes jostled for position in my fevered vision.

The rain which had threatened all day began with a rush and an all-out endeavour to make up for lost time. I returned to the tent. The two occupants were still involved in murmuring sweet nothings, totally oblivious as to what was happening in the world outside. What was happening was that the rain was sheeting down and a forlorn young man was sitting on the wet grass doing his best to keep partially dry under his cycling cape. I sat at the other end of the tent so drenched that further rain hardly mattered.

My eventual appearance at home, drenched and wan, and my subsequent 'bilious attack' was put down to my folly in going out at all on such a day. I got up the following morning shaken and weak, but cured. Thereafter, I ate as little as anyone else in the shop.

The stock was safe from me. From first to last, this eating orgy lasted three weeks and, in this, it took longer than it had done for the others. They were usually sickened within a fortnight.

20. The Common Round

There was a rhythm about working in the shop that varied little from week to week. The store week actually began on a Thursday, but, for convenience, I shall begin on a Monday.

On Monday mornings the new order books and new carbons were laid out in the office under the stairs. Also laid out was a copy of any price changes and/or sales promotions. There were few of either. The prices of some goods did not change during my entire stay. Any price changes were as likely to be down as up. Sales promotions were also thin on the ground. Biscuit week when for every pound she bought, the customer got an ornate tin of biscuits free, was so regular it had become an institution. Anything else we had was intended as a bonus for the customer, rather than an effort to boost sales. The order men were very chary of anything that wasn't sound and value for money. Anything to be noted, was noted by them and they made their get-away as soon as possible. On alternate weeks, those who went out for fortnightly orders collected their much thinner books and left. Thereafter, peace and quiet surged throughout the shop.

The Boss stood on his castle steps watching preparations for the day's work going forward. On the counter next to the Boss's office Mr Routh would prepare to put up a bath of sugar. Nowadays, sugar came in sacks, not 'loafs' as it had done formerly. The sack required was brought down by the warehouseman, who cut the string and poured the contents into the zinc bath standing on two wooden boxes. The bath was the same as those used by miners when they came home from the pit. We never put up a sack of sugar, rice, etc. Always a bath. While the warehouseman was bringing the sugar, an apprentice would fetch the blue sugar bags. Sugar was put up in seven pounds (not half-stones like flour), six-, five-, four-, three-, two- and one-pound bags. These were packed in fixtures in both the front and back shops. Packing fixtures was the work of the apprentices.

Rice, barley, currants and other dry goods were wrapped in squares of paper the colour of which varied according to the product. These huge sheets of sugar paper were cut to shape with the boning knife. When he wasn't on books, Mr Routh almost always 'filled' – that is, he put a quantity of sugar into a bag or a quantity of rice or other product on to a piece of paper and placed this on the counter. The next man picked it off the counter and put it on the scale. With his scoop, he adjusted the quantity, adding or subtracting from it till it weighed the correct amount. Mr Routh's filling was remarkably accurate. Rarely did much adjustment have to be made. The next person wrapped. It was always a joy to me to watch any of the men wrapping. With delicate, skilful, rapid and precise movements, they tucked in the flap, folded and creased the sides and neatly tucked down the result. When rice or similar goods were being put up they were wrapped differently. The two long sides were neatly folded together to form the beginnings of a secure 'packet', one end was given a smart tap so that the packet could be stood on its end, the open end was tucked in and, after any stray grains of rice or barley or whatever was being put up had been swept from the counter into the packet, the other end was tucked in. Sometimes, instead of tucking the ends in they were folded parcel-wise and tied with string. The string was wound round one finger and given a sharp tug. This broke it. Knives and scissors were never used. No matter how many different hands worked on stock, the packets and small parcels resulting were always the same size.

On the week when there were no Hirst fortnightlies to seek, the staff was naturally larger than on the alternate week. After he'd seen everyone working, the Boss would shut himself in his office prepared to deal with any callers he might have. These were usually an isolated traveller or two, or, if they were on the right shift, one or other of the two committeemen assigned to the grocery.

The foreman bent to his task which, on the week we had most staff, was to put in a new window. The window as it stood had three piles of tins, a tall one in the middle balanced by two lesser at either side, rather like towers made by children. The spaces in between were filled with cardboard adverts on their own stands. The foreman directed the apprentice to empty the window, clean it and put the stock away. While this was being done, he went off on an errand of his own. When he returned, he again summoned an apprentice and told him to go down the cellar and bring up cases of stock we had most of. The apprentice did this, opening the cases with a crowbar. The foreman then built three piles of tins, a tall one in the centre and two smaller piles on either side to balance it. In the space between, he put cardboard adverts that stood by themselves.

The usual shop smell of mingled soap, tea, tobacco and cheese was now completely overpowered by the smell of piping-hot water and washing soda as the bacon man washed down his counter and cleansed his machine.

Putting up stock, tidying up and filling fixtures was the order of the day. I worked like fury filling the serving-counter fixtures and, in so doing, made a rod for my own back. To keep me occupied I was banished to the office under the stairs with the invoice book and bidden enter up and extend the invoices, a tedious job hitherto the province of Rose Lynch.

There was a dearth of customers on a Monday. Most were fully occupied with their weekly wash. The Raj served what few there were, but those that came were usually in a tearing hurry, so there was no time for a chat. He filled his time by ruminating over the large yellow check book, meditating on the change in his till or contemplating the near-empty fixtures. He barely recognized my existence and I longed to make contact with him but knew not how to set about it.

One day I had a sudden brain-wave. He was closing his till slowly after watching his customer walk out of the shop when I said, 'It's a pity they didn't make separate compartments for pennies and ha'pennies.' I merely meant this as a friendly overture and to show that my mind did run on serious subjects sometimes. I didn't really give a hoot about the dispositions of the various bits of copper.

He stopped pushing in his till, looked at me, then studied the half-open drawer. 'Yes,' he said slowly. Then, more profoundly, 'Yes.' Then, with even greater depth, 'Yes.' He stared at me fixedly. 'That,' he enunciated slowly and carefully, 'poses several problems. Or, should I say, modifications. Would it be an added improvement to change the actual shape of these compartments? You may have noticed that the copper compartment goes down steeply and ends in a ridge.'

By this time, an influx of customers suddenly and uncharacteristically invaded the shop. The second counter-hand leapt to be of service. The Boss and the foreman were both in the front shop looking our way. It concerned The Raj not at all. I longed to get away to serve as was my duty but those slightly protruding grey eyes of his held me captive and I had less chance of being liberated than the Wedding Guest cornered by the Ancient Mariner.

'In this ridge it is possible that coins might become trapped, although there are none caught there at the moment.' There was a downward inflection to this word that caused me to think he had finished what he wanted to say and I prepared to turn thankfully to a customer.

Unfortunately, the second counter-hand chose that moment to say out of the corner of his mouth, 'The Goss is ucking this ay. Fe's currin.'

The Raj ignored him and renewed his dissertation and, once more, his eyes held me captive. 'And if you inserted a dividing piece of wood, would you make the two compartments of equal . . .?'

The foreman, red-faced, had already come to the counter and was serving. The throat-clearing and hacking cough of the Boss was getting louder. My nerve snapped.

'Yes?' I said sharply to the woman standing nearest.

'I'm being served,' she answered, startled. 'I only want a half of butter.' In my unbalanced state, I went and got her another half-pound.

The lethargy of the afternoon was dispelled when the Hirst fortnightly order men returned with their books, or when trade began to get brisker. The second counter was given over to putting up the orders the men had just brought in. These were usually packed in wooden boxes from which the groceries were taken when they were delivered next day. The boxes were then brought back to the shop.

Three men put up each load; two assembled the goods, then one called out and the other checked that all the things ordered were there. To signify the order was correct, it was signed, the middle bill was torn from the book, placed on the top of the order and weighted down with a tin or package from among the goods checked. The third man placed the order in a box and these were stacked, usually in squares, one square to a load. In the case of the weekly loads and the Newbiggin load, the goods were parcelled in brown paper. Here again, great skill was used in parcelling. However large the order, however unwieldy the goods ordered, flat parcels of uniform depth would result, the order form tucked in in such a way that the name and address showed clearly. Most often, these parcels contained soap, jam and butter, among other things. The soap would be segregated from the rest so that the smell did not permeate any other goods and the jam packed so that the jar did not break.

By five past nine on the particular Tuesday that I have in

mind, as on most, the front shop was pleasantly full of customers who, in an atmosphere of friendly, even jovial, good humour, were being dispatched with the utmost speed and efficiency. At the bacon counter, the bacon man managed to serve, cut bacon, ham and corned beef and, at the same time, make up quantities of provisions for Newbiggin fornightly, ticking them off from a pencilled list written on grey sugar paper already well imprinted with grease. He was assisted in his labours by the second apprentice. Harmony was the keynote. No swearing or the slightest show of annoyance when the bacon man almost fell over one of the shop cats as it scratched among the sawdust near the bacon machine; no shred of irritation when the apprentice practically gave away the knuckle end, to which far too much lean ham still adhered, to old Mrs Orde when it had been earmarked for young Mrs Douglas; nothing but the utmost courtesy on both sides.

At the main counter, only The Raj served at a uniform slow pace. The rest hustled around, even listening to what each other's customers wanted in order to save time. 'I'll get the barley for Mrs Smith when I get me sugar.'

On the second counter, orders were going up at a rate of knots. In his corner Mr Routh assiduously put up rice. He was assisted by Billy Ruddick, the two working quickly together.

'That's champion filling you're doing there, Mr Routh,' Billy said loudly in admiration.

'Aye,' his partner responded modestly and just as loudly. 'It just comes with practice. You're not doing so bad yourself. You're a dab hand.'

'Not as good as you, though,' his companion returned magnanimously. The third apprentice came along to where they were working. As he passed his two senior colleagues he did not joggle the scoop-holding hand of one, nor stumble against the protruding form of the other, pushing him against the zinc bath.

'Can you get by there, young man?' said Mr Routh helpfully, pressing against the counter to allow as much room as his paunch could cater for.

'Thank ye kindly,' the apprentice replied. 'I can manage fine.

Don't trouble yourself, Mr Routh,' he added courteously, as though he'd never ever called him 'Mr Crowth' to get him mad.

In the back shop the Newbiggin load was going up. Jack and another were working at speed and a fair number of orders waited to be wrapped, but, as yet, there was no one to parcel. I was also working in the back shop assisting the oil man. We were in the process of converting the stock of butter banded in wooden casks into a variety of smaller saleable quantities. On any day but Tuesday the oil man (as his name suggests) served paraffin oil, bath brick, donkey stones and blue mottled soap 'round the doors' from his cart which was mostly a fair-sized green tank. On Tuesdays they gave the horse a rest and the oil man had to do a stint in the shop. I was first given this job as his assistant as a stop-gap. The apprentice who normally helped the oil man was away and I was pressed into service. Not understanding the special character of Tuesday, I ploughed on throughout the day, weighing and wrapping, even when there was no one else there. At the end of the day, a record amount of butter had been put up. As I said, sometimes I made a rod for my own back. I was kept on butter and the new tally became the norm.

All this activity was a sight to gladden the heart and eyes of the most exacting manager and buyer – a triumph of corporate effort that a colony of ants might have envied, yet it appeared lost on the one person for whom it was intended. The Boss stood, his hands behind his back, on his little flight of steps, morosely looking out of the shop window. His glum demeanour was at variance with his somewhat festive attire. He was wearing a navy suit (his second best), crisp white shirt, stiff collar, soberly patterned tie and, stretched across his abdomen, his gold Albert with the gold medallion. If appearances were anything to go by, it seemed that something had saddened him and his minions were doing all in their power to alleviate his affliction. Certainly, the conversation of the two putting up rice was loud enough for him to hear, should he desire to. Finally, something in the street caught his eye and, sucking a hollow tooth in preparation for speech, he turned towards the two putters-up of rice.

'You know,' he said to Mr Routh and completely ignoring

Billy, 'having a car is a great responsibility. There's them that thinks it's all pleasure, but they're wrong.'

'Aye,' said Mr Routh respectfully. The choice had been made. Billy's presence was no longer required.

You could never tell just by looking at the Boss which of them it was going to be. Had he said with heavy sarcasm and great wit, 'I've just been watching Dean Swift there,' they would have known he was in a jocular mood and Billy would have been the one to stay. No one could laugh longer or louder or with greater appearance of side-splitting mirth at a joke that wasn't funny than Billy. And he always got his timing right. However, when the boss was in a thoughtful or reminiscent mood, then Mr Routh was the choice. He could remember more (or pretend to) than anyone else and he certainly looked and sounded sagacious and interested, which was what was required.

Released, Billy went into the back shop where he quickly reduced the number of orders waiting to be parcelled.

In the front shop Mr Routh waited for his superior to amplify his thoughts on owning a car. The Boss hadn't yet said enough for him to venture an opinion.

'I'm not saying there's no pleasure to be had. There is. But it's not as much as folk think. We went out for a run on Sunday.' He sucked his teeth and looked to a point beyond the fixtures.

'Aye,' his henchman encouraged. The Boss turned and looked across the street. Mr Routh felt that another remark was expected of him but he was not yet sufficiently confident about which way the wind was blowing. He could only wait. The Boss began to wrap the weighed pounds of rice with deft and expert movements, stacking them neatly for packing into the rice fixture.

'Aye,' he said at last. 'We hadn't been out above half-an-hour when she stopped. Just like that. Stopped.'

'Gerraway,' said the other man in surprise. 'Stopped just like that, eh!' And he clicked his teeth and shook his head in disbelief. He assumed his Boss was talking about the car.

'When I tried to start her up,' went on the narrator, 'she went uh – uh – uh,' and, for his underling's better understanding, he pushed his hands forward and jerked his body against the counter. 'Have you ever been in a car that went like that?'

Mr Routh thought the matter over carefully. 'No,' he said at last with deliberation. 'No, come to think of it, I never have.'

'Then it went ticker, ticker, ticker. Just like that. Ticker. Ticker. Ticker. It nearly had me beat, I can tell you. I had to put me thinking cap on. There's a lot can go wrong with a car.'

'Oh, aye.'

'D'ye know much about the insides of cars?'

The question was carefully considered. 'Well,' Mr Routh said at length, 'I wouldn't call myself an expert exactly.'

'Well, I thought at first it was the Torg, then I tried the plugs and the carburettor. At the finish I thought it must be the magenter had got bunged up. By this time an AA man came along. Of course, he saw at once there was something the matter. I didn't give him the salute. Ye have to give them the salute, you know, Alf, if you're a member. Well, he has a look at it and says "there's not many knows as much about cars as you," he says. "Yer right, it is the magenter. A little bit of petrol'll put her right." So he shoved a bit in the tank. The wife got herself a bit upset. Worried, y'know.'

Mr Routh coughed.

'Womenfolk's like that,' he said soothingly, then, nodding towards the window, 'I think I see the drapery buyer. He's gone again.'

The Boss shook his head. 'I don't think I'll go. I can't really afford the time. There's so much to do.' He said this loud enough for us all to hear. I think it was intended to give us all a fright; to make us think he wasn't going out. He paused and then went on, 'But I suppose I'd better. God knows what they'd send if I wasn't there to say what was wanted.' He finished tucking the second flap into the packet he'd made and tapped it with the side of his hand before putting it with the others. He went into the office and emerged a few minutes later wearing his Dobson hat and his overcoat.

The foreman conjured himself out of the-office-under-the-stairs where he had been engaged in some pursuit of his own and went to the shop door in time to see his over-lord off the premises. He returned to his cubby hole not noticeably bowed down with added responsibility.

This was the day on which the managers and buyers went to select their stock for the coming week from the central premises in Newcastle. We were quite convinced it was as much a social occasion as a task. What the Boss had seen that had moved him to action as he gazed out of the window was the approach of the black saloon (also used for weddings and funerals). It was unthinkable that they should be ready to be taken to Newcastle immediately. They were busy men whose time was valuable, so the driver had to wait. It was also unthinkable that any one of them would have to wait in the car. Whatever their private feelings might be, not one of them was, on the surface, any more important than any other. Long practice ensured that they all arrived at the car at the same time.

Sitting astride his bicycle, balancing himself against a lamp-post on one of the side roads and staring ahead, looking bleak and raw and eating pear drops to keep body and soul together, was the errand boy. Presently, he saw the black saloon with its occupants and, turning the bicycle round, he returned to the shop. When he returned via the back door the customers had been reduced to one. He put his head round the front shop opening to let everyone know he was back. We all carried on with what we were doing. The foreman appeared in the opening between shop and shop, a large silver pocket watch in his hand.

'I'm just going out for a minute to see about the club biscuit orders for Sunday. I'm not happy about them.' Apparently, he was speaking to his watch. The watch did not reply so the foreman returned it to his pocket in pique and left the shop. (Every week we supplied large quantities of Crumpsall cream crackers and American cheese to the local working-men's clubs to encourage a thirst among their members on Sunday mornings.) A few seconds later the bacon man rubbed his hands on a cloth he kept below the bacon machine.

'I'm away along to the butchery,' he said to the second apprentice. 'Look after the counter for a few minutes.' And he, too, left the premises. The second apprentice did stay a few minutes when he followed the second counter-hand into the back shop saying to The Raj as he passed. 'Give us a call if anyone comes.'

The bath of rice had already been abandoned and Rose had just popped across to the drapery. The pulse of the front shop had slowed down so much that it was now scarcely discernible.

The Raj stood along. Hands on hips he turned and surveyed the evaporated-milk fixture. After long consideration he blew on it to remove certain particles of dust. After further thought he bent down and lifted a tin of milk from the opened case on the floor. He regarded it critically, rubbed the bottom and then the top with his elbow. No genie appeared. He placed the tin carefully on the fixture, turning it so that the picture part was to the front. Finally, he stood back to admire his handiwork. Emptying the case would take him the whole day.

In the back shop work had virtually ceased as the errand boy dished out pre-paid hot pies, pasties and sausage rolls brought back in his basket by prior arrangement with a nearby bakery. The hitherto frenzied activity had allowed us to treat the cold air with disdain. Even so, the hot food was more than welcome. The youngest apprentice went into the front shop and cut himself a wedge of cheese which he ate with his pasty.

'I don't know where you put it all,' said the top apprentice.

'He's feeding a tape worm,' said the oil man.

'In the Middle Ages,' I said, 'they would have starved you for three days, strung you upside down, had you hanging about two feet from the ground and put a hot pie on the floor beneath you. The worm would have come out for the pie.'

'Is that the sort of thing they taught you at that toffee-nosed school you went to?' Jimmy asked.

'How, lad,' said the oil man, 'speak when you're spoken to, especially in the presence of your betters.' He turned to me. 'What other tit-bits of information can you give us to add savour to this delicate repast?' he asked.

The food finished, the oil man gave his version of the sabre dance, brandishing the butter knife while two of the apprentices beat out a rhythm on empty biscuit tins. Inevitably, this led to the two of them doing what they called an 'apash dance'. As they finished, Mr Routh returned from wherever he'd been and watched us from a distance.

Billy said in a friendly way, 'That was a heavy furrow you

ploughed there this morning, Mr Routh. He'd run out of petrol. Stupid bugger! His wife gave him hell, so I heard.'

'Aye,' replied the other. 'That's what I thought.' He flushed uncomfortably, possibly because he was neither fish, fowl nor good red meat. He had been a manager. People had regarded him as they regarded the Boss. Now they did and said what they liked when he was there. Also, there was a sort of security in the shop that allowed us to laugh and carry on. Promotion, or non-promotion was out of our hands. Some would be promoted whatever they did – whether they were good grocers or bad ones. Life had not been like that for him.

Then Billy, obviously trying to put him at his ease, said, 'You weren't there the other day when we were putting up beans. He came along and started to wrap. Then he said, "When we went out in the car one Sunday in the Summer and we went into the country and d'ye know the roddegenendrums was lovely." He knew he'd said the wrong word and he looked around everyone as much as to say, "The first one that says I'm wrong gets their holidays in November".'

As he spoke, I had a sudden quick vision of the Boss going home to his wife and saying, 'D'ye know what, I told that lot in the shop today that we'd seen some roddegenendrums, and I looked around and not one of them knew I'd said the wrong word?'

Jimmy who liked to be first with any news that was going, however small, said from his vantage-point near the opening into the front shop, 'The drapery lass is coming.' He also communicated this news to Billy Marks, who had come in to join us.

'Whose turn is it?' they queried among themselves. Being personable and agreeable young men, they took it in turns to serve the drapery lass. The drapery lass was one of four who also took it in turns to come over for threepennyworth of biscuits for a midmorning snack. Tradition had it that before the young lady in question got her biscuits she went down the cellar for a 'bit squeeze'. On this very cold morning a trip into the cellar would be very welcome because of the furnace. Its ancient mechanism was such that it took till dinner-time to get the chill off the air and by closing time at night the warmth was nearing its peak. Myself, I rarely went down the cellar for a warm. The first moment when you opened the heavy door was a delicious but nearly painful experience as a blast of hot air enveloped the upper part of your person and almost knocked you down – but soon, it became too much. In any case, the heat never permeated the bottom half of your body, so after two minutes or thereabouts you had a red face and warm hands – you were hot on the inside, cold on the outside and your feet remained blocks of ice. And then, of course, you had to tear yourself away to go back to the shop or the office, both of which were icy.

Jack went into the front shop and a few minutes later returned with one of the drapery lasses. They made their way down the cellar steps. This was the signal for Billy Marks to positon himself behind the butter casks contained in the decrepit lift then midway between warehouse and cellar. From this position his view of the cellar was completely blocked. He turned this debit into a credit, allowing his imagination free rein.

'Ee, lads,' he said. 'I wish you could see what I can see. He doesn't care where he puts them hands of his. By gox. She'll get her biscuits for nowt this week. Oo. Ah. She deserves a tinful. Chocolate. She'll not want ginger nuts this week . . .' And so it went on. We stood around him laughing. We'd heard it all before. We heard it every week. There was more good-fellowship than humour in our laughter, especially as the reporting was Bowdlerized because I was there.

When the two had emerged brick-red from the furnace and the drapery lass had got her biscuits, I went over to the ladies' cloakroom in the Arcade. There were no facilities for women on our side of the road. By prior arrangement, I met one or two of my friends and we chatted for a while before I returned to the shop. When I got back the lads were grouped round Billy who was telling a funny story. As I went up to the butter counter, they all suddenly roared with laughter.

The oil man looked at his watch.

'Five to twelve!' he said, 'and we haven't finished the halves.' Suddenly, we all became aware of the swift passage of time and worked like fury in an attempt to catch up. The foreman and the bacon man had each returned, a few scattered customers came in and at half-past twelve we closed.

In the early afternoon customers were still very thin on the ground and The Raj soon had the shop to himself. In the back shop, four of the man were singing 'Lily of Laguna' in harmony. They sang very well indeed. When they'd finished, Billy Marks, gave us his rendering of 'Three Old Ladies'. We heard of the adventures of Elizabeth Porter (the vicar of Chichester's daughter), of the travails of Elizabeth Vickers (who, predictably, had trouble with her knickers) and of the exploits of Elizabeth Hunt (of whose difficulties the less said, the better).

It wasn't all singing and jokes and daft carry on. Sometimes we had a serious discussion. I really liked these, but I never took part, being happier to listen. During a discussion, for the most part, we kept on working. One day, the participants talked of the possibility of war. Normally, I shut my ears to this type of debate. I just didn't want to know. The thought of another Great War, but worse, and the fact that my brother would be old enough to go, was more than I could contemplate. This time, however, I was listening.

'What we really need,' said Billy at one point, 'is a first-class arbitrator.'

'If war does come,' said the oil man in admiration, 'you'd make a first-class officer.'

In the far corner an apprentice was changing over the vinegar casks. I went up to him.

'What's an arbitrator?' I asked quietly.

'Now how the hell would I know!' he said. 'I'm not an encyclopedia.'

A little while later, while I was working on my own, Billy came up to me and putting his hand on my shoulder said, 'An arbitrator is an intermediary between two conflicting parties. When two factions hold entirely opposite views, an arbitrator tries to find common ground to bring them together. If we had skilled arbitrators, wars might be stopped.'

I was extremely appreciative of the fact that he'd thought my query worthy of notice and that he'd taken the first quiet opportunity to remove a modicum of my ignorance.

The oil man returned.

'Lads,' he said. 'It's just after half-past two.' We were alarmed and suddenly became serious. Before long, the foreman came in and walked over to the counter. When he saw him coming, one of the lads flicked over some pages in the order book. The foreman peered at the page.

'You should have been further on than that,' he said. He came over to us. 'How many have you done?' he asked. 'All but three,' the oil man said, not looking at him. I wrapped furiously keeping my eyes down.

For the remainder of the afternoon we worked like automata, speaking only when necessary. The front shop started to fill with customers and the counterhands served at speed so that no one would be taken off a job to help them out. At half-past three the Boss turned red of visage and sour of mien. He seemed to have developed a warped view of all mankind (and womankind). He called the foreman and that gentleman went in with a long sheet of paper on which was written the activities of the staff who had been in the shop that day, as fine a piece of fiction as was to be found in any library.

The number of customers increased and I was transferred to the counter. We were hopelessly behind on the butter counter so I made a detour into the back shop for every item that I might wrap a few more ones and twos. Billy also helped, wrapping parcels and butter alternately. Finally, quarter-past five arrived and, one by one, we reached the end of our appointed tasks. Currants, lentils, rice, sugar and beans were up and a bath of barley started, the bacon orders were up, the Newbiggin load was up and the quota of butter needed to see us through the week was neatly stacked in the cellar. At half-past five we closed for the night.

Wednesday was early-closing day. It was also tick day, the one day in the week when credit was given. The second counter was the tick counter, the principal counter being kept for cash customers. The shop opened before nine and when we got there, there was already a sizeable crowd waiting. It was a very good-humoured crowd – it had to be. Even with every available person serving, it was difficult to keep pace.

One of the time-consuming factors was that on the tick counter we *had* to make proper bills out. We were supposed to do this on the other counter also, but we almost never did, being content to scribble the amounts on any available scrap of paper, count the number of goods and the number of amounts to see that they tallied and then get the total. On the tick counter, however, the bills had to be pasted on to the existing weekly or fortnightly order and charged.

We had a secret 'black list' and we were supposed to check with this. It was pasted on the side of the pill cabinet and we'd been told to glance at this surreptitiously. When I served my first tick customer, I asked her her name and went up to the pill cabinet to glance at the side.

'You needn't look at the black list,' my customer screeched down the shop. 'Me name's not on.' Everyone in the shop roared with laughter. My cheeks were on fire but I managed a grin.

Many were the sallies and often loud was the laughter that characterized tick mornings. That the jokes were whiskered with age didn't seem to matter. As the morning progressed the order men returned from their rounds and they, too, joined those serving at the tick counter till, finally, the last customer had been allowed through the now-locked door and we were free to go home.

Thursday was the day that all staff, the oil man excepted, worked in the shop. The weekly loads had to be put up. The Newbiggin load would have been delivered the previous day so that the central area of the back shop was free to receive the stacked parcels. The area in front of the first and second counters was also cleared. Two teams worked in the front shop and one in the back putting up orders. The bacon man toiled to supply the counter and the loads. As soon as a load was finished, Rose had to stick any tick bills on with Gloy and write in the amount. She did this in between serving milk checks. Then the book had to be extended, totalled and checked and, finally, each book had to be entered, bill by bill, in another book. This last was done by Rose.

Thursday morning on the counter was every bit as busy as Wednesday's tick counter had been. But on this morning there were no time-worn, superannuated jokes, no laughter, assumed or otherwise. Many of the customers were 'on Relief'. Before they had come to us, they had stood for their Relief notes, answering the most searching questions about their non-existent finances put by the man who would ultimately decide how much they should have. They were given a long white piece of paper on which was written the things they could choose from and the amount they could have money-wise. The goods were the necessities of life – flour, margarine, sugar, tea, corned beef or whatever – all of the cheapest quality. In this respect, we served our Relief customers well. We sold no inferior goods. When the Boss made his excursions into the central premises, he chose only the best quality. Anything else to us was 'ket'. The only thing we sold which could be termed poorer was a line of biscuits which we sold at 6*d.* a pound, but we did not sell many of those and we often dissuaded customers from buying them.

Relief recipients were allowed no luxuries on these notes, but many of the assistants were lenient. By far the most popular counter-hand in this field was Jack, although he did not always serve. His generous heart was easily touched and he never refused to give an ounce of tobacco or a packet of Woodbines, putting these commodities down as blue mottled soap or blacking. Other goods disguised as Zebo or Brasso were tinned pineapple chunks and our cheapest mixed-fruit jam. A number of those serving refused to give tobacco in any form but relented over the chunks. It is interesting to note that black lead to clean the fire was designated an 'essential', while treats in the form of tinned fruit or soothing tobacco were not.

Some gave only what was on the note and, initially, so did I. But, one day, a girl I recognized came in. She couldn't have been much more than 17, a scant three years older than I. I'd seen her once or twice all bright and jaunty with her hair bleached and permed, her pale cheeks reddened to match her lips, hanging on to the arm of her lad and teetering along on high heels. Now, she looked thin, poorly clad, her bleached hair growing out. She'd 'had to get married' and they were on Relief. It was her first note. She made no attempt to claim her turn and Jack had to make a deliberate effort to get her to hand her note over. She asked for a large tin of pears, a tin of evaporated milk, two jellies, some jam . . .

'I couldn't give you all that, pet, even if I wanted to,' Jack said. 'That's not what the notes are for. You've got to buy things to help feed you through the week. Things like bread and . . . and . . . You have learned to cook, haven't you?'

She shook her head.

'Let's start again,' he said. 'Flour?'

She shrugged.

'Give me what you think,' she said in a voice devoid of all emotion.

I felt a sudden surge of hot anger, but I couldn't explain why. It had nothing to do with Relief notes or the people concerned with them. It had more to do with feelings. The feelings inside her that had made her bleach her hair and pinch her feet in high-heeled shoes was the same thing that had brought her to this state. I felt she had been wronged somehow.

Till that moment, Relief customers had just been something else I had to learn. Seeing the change circumstances had wrought on this girl, I felt for them all and I, too, slipped in a tin of chunks in lieu of something evocative of hard work. When the Boss or the foreman were not in the vicinity, like Jack I took to slipping in a few pear drops buckshee, if I knew there were children.

Round about eleven o'clock the first book would be ready for extending and totalling and I would be sent to the office. In warm weather, the room was clammy and airless, in cold weather, chilled – until just after lunch when the central heating was climbing to its zenith after which time we were almost as hot as the furnace itself.

As I became more adept and accurate, the tense atmosphere began to slacken and we indulged in spasmodic conversation as we totalled. We also sang. With very little persuasion Mr Routh would sing 'The Moon Doth Raise Her Lamp Above'. He had a very pleasant singing voice. After the first rendition, we joined in in harmony. At least Bobby did. Having a very poor singing voice, I added nothing to the harmony, but I sang just the same. Then Mr Routh would often sing 'Speak, Speak, Speak to me

Thora.' The nearer we got to five-thirty, the less we talked and sang. One of the perks for doing books, as far as Bobby was concerned, was that his own load was dealt with as soon as it came in, thus giving him a good chance of getting away early next day.

On Friday morning there was a terrific rush to see that all was completed as soon as possible. The men with loads would get fidgety about the change coming down from the general office. This change provided for their floats. Once that was down and checked they could go, unless, of course, their books were not finished. This involved much neck-breathing-down as the order men in question saw armies of insurance agents and tally men carting away cash that should have been theirs.

Once the last book was finished; it was back to the counter for me. The hours on Fridays and Saturdays were longer than those of other days, but they passed quickly, we were so busy.

This was a very happy time, as far as I was concerned. After Billy's explanation about the meaning of 'arbitrator' we some-times walked home together. He had been to Morpeth Grammar School. We talked of the subjects he'd done. He had also been to the Co-operative college and he told me about his time there. Unfortunately, I did not ask him how he had gained his place. We often laughed together. We found a great deal to laugh about and to discuss, and I had much to ask him. It was a great joy reading a book and then finding there was someone with whom to share it. The tenor of our conversation was different from the backchat of the shop.

Improving one's education by reading at home is no doubt commendable, but there are drawbacks. For instance, when you come across something you really don't understand your only recourse is to the dictionary or the encyclopedia. This is time-consuming and often frustrating. Sometimes I read something which contradicted what I'd been taught, or blew sky-high convictions I'd held since childhood. On these occasions there was no one to say, 'Yes, but you must read X, Y, or Z on the subject, and see what it has to say.' Thus, to have someone like Billy as a mentor was a joy. My horizons spread ever wider. The road ahead was exciting. My dreams took wings and I grew ever-more ambitious. I have never really put a ceiling on my dreams and ambitions when I've had them, nor have I thought I must travel one path only. All paths are exciting, even when they lead to dead-ends. Even then, on the return journey it is just possible you might see something you missed the first time you passed.

I'd had another visit from the education secretary to whose method of breaking news I had now become accustomed. I had taken just about all the examinations I could. I should now try to get to college. He didn't say which college nor how I was to get there. (On one of my summer schools, I met a young man whose society had sent him to Oxford.) In the euphoria of the moment I did not ask. But that did not matter. It seemed possible that I could go and who else could I go to for help and advice but Billy? I saw the future open up. College and then who knew? Co-operation in a much wider field. Perhaps even setting up a Co-op centre of learning similar in character to the mining school the coal company had set up for its employees in Ashington to which students within travelling distance came – a mining school that had made a name for itself as young men who showed promise and were willing to work could enrol, attend, take examinations and finally become colliery managers regardless of family status.

It was a shock, therefore, to go to work next morning and learn that Billy was leaving. He had not mentioned the possibility to me, nor did I consider this omission unusual. He had been off for the interview and, though I missed him and had a feeling everyone else knew where he was, I did not ask. The unwritten rules by which children are brought up often linger past childhood. You should not ask personal questions; you will be told as much as it is good for you to know. Thus, I did not ask for any details from Billy, or anyone else for that matter. I relied on shop gossip which might or might not have been reliable. I gathered that he had been appointed as a full-time education officer with another Society. Why, if other Societies had full-time education officers, could not we? Why was it necessary for him to leave? He belonged to our Society. Why, on the moving staircase of promotion, did he have to stay on one step and take his turn? Everyone in the shop recognized his merits and ability.

They all recognized that if he wanted to get on, he would have to leave. I found it all very puzzling and bewildering, but Billy was eleven or twelve years older than I and I felt I could not bring this very personal matter up with him. Neither, in the face of his changed status, did I feel I could ask questions about college.

It might seem strange that I did not ask these simple questions of the people with whom I worked or whom I met regularly. Uncle Lance had, himself, been to the Co-operative college and, with hindsight, I know he would have been more than willing to help me towards achieving my goal. But I only know this with hindsight.

Generally speaking, all men, from the way they were treated at home, were equated with authority. Very often, whatever little joys or troubles had ruffled the domestic scene, when the man of the house (or any man of the house) came in from work, all had to be calm and peaceful while he had his meal, his bath and his pipe. This quiet and calm atmosphere (necessary, no doubt) had to persist for several hours if the worker was on night shift. Also, most often, if a child wanted something, it was the mother who was first applied to. She would word the request in such a way as to make it more acceptable and approach the father at a time she felt would be most opportune. All this helped, in a veiled way, to distance children from the adult male members of the family and to set a pattern for male children to fall into as they grew to adulthood.

Similarly, however hard a woman was working, she had to stop to attend to the domestic needs of the men of the household when they came in, thus reinforcing the idea that what women did was of less importance when it was compared with what men did.

Again, adult authority was often unpredictable and confusing to a child who lacked the background or logic to work out why A was the result when B was confidently expected.

My parents did their best to treat my brother and me in the same way. One Sunday afternoon we had been detailed to wash up the tea things. After we had set up the obligatory howls of protest, we were left to get on with the work, me standing on a stool enveloped in my mother's overall doing the washing and

Billy, minus his jacket, his tie tucked in and his Sunday trousers protected by a clean tea-towel, doing the drying. Once we'd started, it proved to be a friendly and companionable project. The cups, spoons, knives and some cake plates had to be properly washed while only bits of the saucers needed washing and, consequently, drying. We held the plates up to the light, examining them critically to mark off the areas smeared by butter, jam or cake, so that we might not wash and dry more than was absolutely necessary.

As we scrutinized one plate being held up to the light and looking at the changing pattern made by the sunlight, the scullery door opened and we turned to smile at Uncle Jack who stood on the threshold with Aunt Jean behind him. He did not smile. He stood stock-still, and pointed a finger at the towel protecting my brother Billy's Sunday garb.

'*Get that off*,' he said. 'This minute. And don't *ever* let me see that again. *Never. Washing dishes is women's work.*'

Nothing loth, Billy did as he was told and disappeared through the scullery door and into the room, Aunt Jean and Uncle Jack following. I waited for him to come back, as I knew he would, because my mother did not take kindly to having her authority usurped. But the next thing I saw was Billy rushing to freedom, putting his jacket on as he went and crashing the door behind him. I finished my task totally bewildered. When I went into the room to report, all four were sitting in a semi-circle laughing uproariously as Uncle Jack and Aunt Jean between them were relating an incident. No one saw that I was there. I sidled out of the room and sat on the stairs, dismayed and confused by what had happened. Normally, I'd have sat in the room listening to their talk and their laughter, I so loved seeing them enjoy themselves. But I could not, because a new, unsettling factor had come into my life and I could not reconcile myself to it. It did not occur to me that my mother had never heard Uncle Jack's order, but had assumed the dishes were finished, we had taken so long. Her customary inspection did not take place because of our visitors.

Similarly at school. In the class where I was bidden remain in the 'B' section, I worked unceasingly to remain top, in fact if not in position. I did this for two reasons. I hoped the teacher would put me in the 'A' section. I was afraid that if I lost my place, I would be moved down and not allowed to move up again.

About a month after the incident itself, I was absent from Monday till Thursday. I begged to be allowed to return to school on the Friday, the day the tests were done, and, except for composition where the previous week's marks prevailed, marks were allocated.

The composition was written during the first period of Friday afternoon, but its preparation began on the Monday before, when the title was written on the board: 'A Letter'. Then followed a lesson on how to set out a letter and the necessary spellings, to be learned that night. On Tuesday, suggestions were asked for and given for the first paragraph. The acceptable suggestions were written up on the board, punctuation marks and spellings noted and drummed home. On Wednesday, paragraph two was similarly treated and, on Thursday, paragraph three and the ending. By the time Friday came the subject was fairly well fixed in the minds of the class and if 50 almost identical compositions were written, then it must be remembered they had to be taken home by the teacher, marked, and every mistake noted and commented on. On Monday morning, the marks were given out, retribution exacted, and corrections done. The mark formed the basis of that week's test marks.

Returning on Friday, I had missed the preparation.

'Now don't forget,' said the teacher, 'I want a nice, newsy letter about what's happening. All about your friends and family and what you think will interest them.'

I thought a bit and decided to write my letter to Auntie Isa, the aunt whose name I was most confident about spelling correctly.

Daer anty Izer,
    Ther is this man and he has this dog and he brgs it wakin down oru strete in the colry skeem all the way from the hirst wy in the wied werld wuld aynyoen want to wak a dog in the colry skeem from the hirst well his wyf dyed a few weeks bakc and this womn father down coms to the col

huose evrye tiem he cums al dresd up and las weke she ast him in is that not a disgrays and his wyife not cold in her grayv yet. meyunkelkit has got a bad kevil agian the thrid tiem runen and he wrks wet up to his oggstus and sumtiems he ony gets there shifts in it taeks them all ther tiem to manig and meyunkelandra has a beet bakc hees on the sikc but he says with god swil they manig thats beceuas he is a brethren but he geos to the cherch becuas ther arnet meny brethrens in Ashington to pas for a brethren yuo havent to go to conserts or the pickshers or the gozy or a soshul or go ferzfutin or drinkc bere or wien not evn docter wattsins toynk stowor go to the clerb or the perb or play cards or swear. not meny peeopel in Ashington can pas so ther arent meny brethrens so they have no cherch I thinkc meyunkelandra is the ony wone so he sits at the bakc beceuras uor cherch is to soft for him. wel I mus cloes now to cacth the poast yuoer loving nesce lLinda.

On Monday morning, as we filed in, I saw that our compositions were lying in a pile on the desk as usual, but, today, one book was lying open. Even from the back I knew it was mine because my book was the only one backed in wallpaper (the off-white side), all the others were backed in brown paper. I could only conclude my effort was going to be read out to the class, as sometimes happened. Anyway, the great, the thrilling thing was, it was lying on the top. That could only mean one thing. I had a good mark.

We had only just said the Lord's Prayer and were sitting up, hands behind backs while the register was being called, when Miss Dixon came in. She walked over to the teacher's desk, and, as she called names, the teacher nodded towards my book. Miss Dixon started reading and she smiled, then she laughed. The teacher stopped calling the register and pointed with her pen as if to say, 'Is that what you're laughing at?' and together they read a bit more silently and laughed a bit more. I was completely puzzled. It couldn't be my composition. I hadn't said anything funny. But it certainly had a white back, and the others were brown. Then Miss Dixon wrinkled her nose a little bit. She had her finger on a word and the teacher said, 'First Footing' and I knew then it *was* my book. The class was also puzzled, looking at each other uncertainly, undecided whether or not they were expected to join in the joke, whatever it was. I didn't understand but I was perfectly prepared to join in the fun. In the meantime, I gave myself up to wondering what mark I'd got. Certainly not less than eight. Nine, possibly. I smiled inside at the thought and the pleasure it brought. Finally, Miss Dixon picked up the book and still laughing, took it away while the teacher finished her register.

The first lesson after playtime was the one to give out the books and the marks. I sighed with inward happiness more than once during scripture, mental arithmetic and arithmetic.

When we filed back into the classroom I sat down with the rest and waited. My book had been returned and it now lay at the bottom of the pile. This was consistent with the good wine being left till last. One by one the books were dealt with – the beaming smile for the nines and eights, the you-must-try-harder for the sevens and sixes, the you-did-not-listen-to-one-word-I-said for the fives and fours and the active, eloquent strap for the threes, twos and ones. One book remained.

'And now,' the teacher said dramatically, 'I want you to look at this,' and, with a theatrical flourish she held my opened book up for inspection.

The class responded with a gasp of delighted horror.

My composition had a bad case of red-ink poisoning. It was a mass of tiny, stinging red-ink lacerations. There were red rings of inflammation round the blue-black bruises caused by the overflow from my generous nib. Down the margin, red-ink blood streamed, pink and fresh from the heart.

I gripped the edge of the form and set the muscles of my face to combat the unexpected onslaught and keep back the tears.

'No proper beginning.' Concerted, surprised catching of breath. 'One hundred and seven spelling mistakes. Most of them careless.' 'Eee.' Lower lips caught between teeth. A relaxing of the atmosphere. 'No capital letters.' Wide-eyed in-drawn breaths. 'Only one full stop.' Cautious, hunched shoulders and wary looks to either side. 'Seven crossings-out.' Bolder looks to right and left. Open-mouthed gasps. 'No proper ending.'

The turning of heads to look at the culprit. This was turning out to be as good as the last lesson before the Christmas holidays. I did what I could to smile, aware, even as I did so, of the two large, slightly crooked front teeth, growing into the gap in the front of my mouth. I must have looked funny, too. The class was invited to take part in a lighthearted discussion as to what my punishment ought to be. I did not hear what they said.

So when Billy left the store, it was a blow to me personally. Here was a man, an adult, to whom I could talk freely and who listened to what I had to say. He did not think it strange that I should be interested in books and learning to the exclusion of almost everything else and that my goal was to attend college some day, some time. There were very few to whom I'd confided these ambitions of mine. Without exception those to whom I did said, 'Wait till Mr Right comes along. You'll change your tune then.'

We talked together and we laughed together, but the things we laughed about were not the obvious jokes. They were smiles rather than laughs and they arose spontaneously from the subjects we talked about. Wit rather than humour.

With him gone, I felt I was in no-man's land – or rather, no-woman's land – as far as college was concerned. I had some idea that Latin was required and that the books one read were large, erudite and practically unintelligible.

I managed to get a book on Latin and large, erudite books from the store library. They were certainly old enough and dusty enough. Who had been last to use them I could not conceive. The library was extremely loth to lend them to me. That I simply wanted to read them was regarded with suspicion. For what purpose? How could I say? Finally, I carted them home. Neither they nor the Latin Grammar were easy. It wasn't the Latin I had learned at school and I could not wade through the books I'd borrowed. I returned them, largely unread. A male clerk took them from me. He twisted his face slightly as he held them.

'What were they about?' he asked.

I couldn't tell him I didn't know, after my determination to borrow them.

'Well,' I said, my mind racing. 'Have you heard of Gibbon?'
'No.'

'Well, they're after that fashion. I took a deep breath. 'They . . .'

'You needn't go on. I have work to do. I was curious, that's all. I still am. I can't imagine what sort of mind you have to be able to read that sort of stuff and enjoy it when you could be going out and having a good time.'

21. Your Country Needs You More Than The Store

With the coming of the Second World War, naturally things changed. In my case I plunged into Civil Defence with a great deal more enthusiasm than expertise.

I became an ambulance driver.

My parents had bought a car and, after my father and then my brother had passed their tests, I, being old enough, was permitted to try. Individual car owners were becoming more numerous in Ashington but they were not yet very thick on the ground. Girl drivers were a rarity. Nevertheless, I was allowed to procure a provisional licence. At the same time I had applied to take a test a little over three weeks later. This was so that I could get three tests in on the one licence. If I couldn't get through on the third attempt, the obvious conclusion would be reached.

Fred Young, whose undoubted skill in this field was proven, taught me to drive. At that time he was an ambulance driver and worked shifts which meant there was limited opportunity for driving instruction because he also worked overtime. However, it was while he was on a week's holiday with us that I got much of my tuition from him. For the rest, my driving instruction took place on the then very quiet roads leading to Lynemouth, Alnmouth, Widdrington and Ulgham. I drove to Newcastle and back on the night before my test was due. Workmates of my father, hearing of this, felt they ought to drop in at our house to give some friendly advice on how to outwit the examiner, for, it appeared, his mission in life was to catch out unwary learner drivers and those same examiners were getting more wily by the day. It wasn't actually people who had a car and who had taken a test who came. It was those whose friends had undergone the ordeal and had suffered so much that they could scarcely speak of it. And I wasn't spoken to direct; I had to pick up the information as it pulsed its way through the atmosphere.

'I'll tell you what it is, Arch, you've got to have all your buttons on nowadays when you go for a test. Not like it was when you went. They're out to catch you. Chap I know did everything right. Never put a foot wrong. He failed. You know why? The examiner says, as they were just going along, "Have you got a cigarette?" and, of course, he puts his hand in his pocket for his tabs. Failed. Another chap did everything perfect. The examiner told him. He said, "You've done everything perfect," but he failed 'cos, you see, the examiner asked him for a light, and not thinking, he put his hand in his pocket for his matches. It's easy done. You got to be on your toes. They're out to catch you, make no mistake about that. The thing is, you should leave your tabs and matches at home or give them to somebody to look after while you're on the test . . .'

'But I don't smoke.'

'. . . but even then, Arch, they've got it in for you. D'you know Pigeon Joe, him that lives at the Hirst? His missus fliggied off with one o' them chaps come to work here from down South and then she wanted him to take her back but he wouldn't because his sister had come to look after him and she managed all right. Well, the daughter married a fella from Manchester or some of them places and his cousin got himself a car and when he went for his test everybody said he couldn't miss but pass – but he failed. D'you know what happened, Arch? The examiner said, when they were boolin' along a straight road, "Just look at that fella on the other side," in Manchester, of course, Arch. They don't talk the way we do. And he did and he failed him. And he couldn't miss but pass. So, you see, it's the same wherever you go. You wouldn't believe the tricks they've got up their sleeve. And when they've got a young bit lass in the car it makes your hair stand on end to think what might happen. I'll tell you what it is, Arch, if it was me I wouldn't be letting any lass of mine anywhere near an examiner or a car. They just aren't up to it. But, of course, I mean it in good part. I'm not trying to tell you your business. You know that, Arch. You know me. But I just felt I had to warn you.'

Unfortunately, Fred had a very busy morning and didn't get away on time. Although he did without his lunch, we arrived in Newcastle 20 minutes late for my test at three o'clock. I wasn't made any more confident by the fact that I stalled the engine in the centre of the crossroads on Northumberland Street. I went into the office with all the fortitude of a thoroughly scared rabbit and apologized for my late arrival, quite prepared to find that my test had been cancelled.

The examiners I have met during my lifetime are legion, from the St John's First Aid examiner, a pit-man due shortly on night shift, to the sage professor stooping under the weight of academic honours. Some there are of benign, angelic appearance who urge you to take your time while others have honed their eyes to steel points and their teeth to razors, all the better to eat you with. By the same token, I have known those who radiate approval and smile commendation, give abysmal marks, while others, who snarl (metaphorically) as you try their patience and waste their time, give high honours.

This examiner was a prince among inquisitors. He brushed

my apology aside, saying he was sure I could not help being late and I must not worry, he had ample time before his next appointment. He fully restored what confidence I had and I drove, turned, reversed, did a three-point turn, stopped suddenly and answered questions as requested.

'Have you any idea of the speed at which you were travelling most of the time?' he asked when we'd finished.

'As fast as I could within the speed limit,' I answered. 'I was hoping I would not make you late for your next appointment.'

'I thought that was the reason,' he said. 'You were travelling at 28. Other than that, you did very well. You're going to make a good driver.'

'You mean . . .?'

'I mean you've passed.'

I didn't know how I was going to tell them.

I hadn't put in much more practice when war was declared.

The second air-raid warning we had (the first was on the day war was declared) happened on a Tuesday. What occasioned it, we did not know, for nothing besmirched the morning sky, but we all darted to our posts, those of us who had posts to dart to. The shop was emptied of customers – they were sent scurrying to their homes – and the staff who had no specific duties went down the cellar. We were not the only ones to jump to action. At the pit, the coal lorries were quickly denuded of their coal and taken to the First Aid post to be rechristened as ambulances and driven by amateur drivers, of whom I was one. (This practice did not last long. The lorries were replaced by cars lent for the duration.)

When the all-clear sounded we returned to our duties after having discussed why the alert had been given in the first place. Naturally, the war had interfered with our work routine and this the foreman explained to the Boss on his return. The Boss listened in amazement, his incredulity growing with every word, his face glowing like a warning beacon.

'You mean to say,' he spluttered, 'you closed the shop! And pushed the customers out!! And went down the cellar!!!' He lifted his considerable voice and bellowed, 'In future this shop doesn't close, air raid or no air raid. If the bombs start dropping near enough, you can get under the counter till they stop. But work goes on. And before you go tonight, the work that should have been done today gets finished. And don't let me hear the word overtime from anybody.'

Ration books and ration coupons became my province. At first, goods were plentiful, but gradually the quantities of goods coming in became smaller and some items disappeared altogether. Choice also disappeared as customers had to take what was available, rather than what they wanted. Tinned stuff that had hitherto lain unwanted now sold like hot cakes. In the end, customers took what they were given.

The actual work pattern of the shop did not change. Goods were still put up and orders taken and sent out. The number of our customers remained stable and we held a large quantity of ration books from which I cut the coupons as needed. Allocating deliveries of things like chocolate and biscuits which never came in quantities anything like enough to go round, brought problems and, inevitably, there were charges of favouritism. As far as we could, we gave out 'extras' on a rota basis – Weekly One one time, Weekly Two the next, and so on.

The ethos of the shop did change in other ways, however. The young men were leaving. Mr Dunn (the Boss) retired and Mr Joe Miles took his place. Whereas Mr Dunn had tended to turn a blind eye if it suited his purpose, Mr Miles kept both eyes wide open all the time, preferring to keep to the letter of the law, rather than its broad principles. Mr Coxon was replaced by Mr

Ralph Robson as foreman.

To replace the young men leaving, or about to leave, a number of young girls were appointed.

Although I missed my unique position among the men, I was more than compensated by the presence of so many girls, never having worked with girls of my own age.

In the all-male stronghold, new apprentices coming in did so singly. Thus, they could be treated singly and put in their places in the hierarchy of things and, in this way, they were initiated and became 'blood brothers' with a loyalty to each other – my brother, right or wrong. Shortly after I joined the shop on a Saturday night just before closing, the three youngest apprentices got me under the shop tap and scrubbed my face, getting my hair wet into the bargain. One or two older men stood around undecided whether or not to stop the caper; certainly to see that it didn't go too far. It was a painful experience from which I emerged red-faced and with dripping front hair. I neither cried nor complained. It was part of the inexplicable structure of things. The girls did not feel it necessary that any ordeal should be undergone to cement feelings of sisterhood. We were there by accident, and to do a job.

It seemed as if the girls swamped the men, robbing them of some of their colour. One day, I wondered how they would react to being asked to do just one of the things I had been required to do as a beginner. I chose the girl I thought most likely to do it in good part.

'I've decided to put up some little fixtures to take these coupons,' I said. 'Be an angel and mosey along to the butchery for a Long Stand. You're more likely to get one there than anywhere else.'

She came back in tears. I had played a stupid, childish, dirty trick on her and she was extremely offended. There was little I could do or say to soothe her feelings.

There were factions and cliques among us girls, too – something which had never happened in the days of male supremacy. Even when they had differences of opinion, the men tended to stay together.

Engaging young girls only increased the number of leavers.

When my turn came, parting was no sweet sorrow. Leaving had become almost commonplace and was no more marked than our going off on holiday had been, except that there was always a whip-round. I got 19s. (95p).

I had started on a Thursday and I left tidily on a Wednesday. It was a different sort of Wednesday from the one I'd first known. There were fewer tick customers. But the change had been imposed by external circumstances. Of itself, the store and its ethos had not changed. The foreman was already putting his coat on when I came to the office under the stairs for mine.

I dawdled.

'Hurry up, pet,' he said as he went out to try the doors in the back shop.

In the seconds that were left to me, I looked round the impassive office. It had not changed any more for me than it had done for the others who had left over the years. Like the shop, it remained what it had always been, a solid Victorian building of solid Victorian worth and outlook and it appeared to have every intention of staying that way.

Both the Co-operative movement and Ashington had developed from small beginnings in the 1840s, a tiny shop and a hole in the ground. The movement had grown apace at an international level because its ideas and the way they were implemented were right in both time and place. Ashington had also grown apace, but at a parochial level. Like countless other mining communities, it was a village, but it became paramount among villages in the area, the one to which others, even those of grander lineage, gravitated. Small wonder that the principles of the patriarchs of both developments remained steadfast, if a little blinkered.

There was nothing in the small, dark office to say, 'Linda was here.' Had I gouged my name on the desk to relieve the boredom of doing invoices, I'd have left more impression.

As I walked home pondering the way things had turned out, or hadn't turned out, what I did not realize was that I'd had a long gestation in the womb of a close and loving community, with the inhibitions this provided. In less than 48 hours, in Fenham Barracks, the umbilical cord would be severed, after which – long after which – I would agree with J.R. Lowell.

'Only by unlearning wisdom comes.'